Sanctification

Sanctification

Transformed Life

Banner Mini-Guides
Key Truths

David Campbell

THE BANNER OF TRUTH TRUST

THE BANNER OF TRUTH TRUST

Head Office
3 Murrayfield Road
Edinburgh, EH12 6EL
UK

North America Office
PO Box 621
Carlisle, PA 17013
USA

banneroftruth.org

© The Banner of Truth Trust, 2018
First published 2018
Reprinted 2020

ISBN
Print: 978 1 84871 826 5
EPUB: 978 1 84871 875 3
Kindle: 978 1 84871 886 9

*

Typeset in 10/14 pt Minion Pro
at the Banner of Truth Trust, Edinburgh

Printed in the USA by
Versa Press, Inc.,
East Peoria, IL

To
the congregation of
North Preston Evangelical Church
with appreciation for
all your prayers and encouragement
during the writing of this book

Contents

	Introduction	ix
1.	Fitting It into the Bigger Picture	1
2.	Holy God, Holy People	9
3.	Sanctification: the Work of God	17
4.	Looking at Jesus	25
5.	How It All Begins	33
6.	Plain Sailing?	41
7.	Time To Get the Knife Out	49
8.	Expectations	57
9.	The All-Important Setting	65
10.	Not in Isolation	73
11.	Blessings along the Way	81
12.	Reality Check	89
13.	Finished at Last!	97
	Further Reading	105

Introduction:
God's Glorious Salvation

Transformed. It's a strong word. But not too strong. For transformation is what sanctification is all about. In particular, of our hearts and lives. Sanctification is a work of God that takes place inwardly and shows itself outwardly. It changes the people we are and in doing so changes the way we live. And the result is nothing less than a transformation – right from the very beginning, increasingly as the work continues, and eventually to an unimaginable degree when it is finished.

Transformed is also a Bible word. In what is a key text on sanctification, the apostle Paul speaks about how 'we all, with unveiled face, beholding the glory of the Lord, are being *transformed* into the same image from one degree of glory to another' (2 Cor. 3:18). Similarly, in what is another key text on sanctification, he says to us, 'Do not be conformed to this world, but be *transformed* by the renewal of your mind' (Rom. 12:2). Transformation is the correct category for us to use as we think about the difference that sanctification makes.

And then there is the underlying Greek word. What a window this opens on the subject! It is the word from which we get our English word *metamorphosis*. I always associate it with butterflies. Maybe you do too. What begins as a caterpillar crawling on a leaf ends as a beautiful winged butterfly. In the Greek New Testament it is the word that is used of our Saviour when he was transfigured before his disciples (Mark 9:2). So too in the texts from Corinthians and Romans referenced above.

Metamorphosis. The *Oxford English Dictionary* defines it as 'a complete change in the appearance, circumstances, condition, character of a person.' He or she has been transformed! And as God begins, carries on, and completes his sanctifying work in believers the result is similarly radical and far-reaching. As we shall see.

DAVID CAMPBELL

Preston, 2018

1

Fitting It into the Bigger Picture

When a war or an earthquake devastates a city, recovery is multi-faceted. Roads, power lines, houses, public buildings, water supply and sewerage all need to be renewed – everything that made the city functional; everything that enhanced it. It is no different with salvation. The devastation wrought by the entrance of sin is deep and widespread. As a consequence, making all things new requires the work of God on a number of different fronts.

Surveying the damage

Take the relationship between ourselves and God, for example. Sin has broken it. When our first parents, Adam and Eve, were made nothing gave them greater pleasure than the company of God. But not after they sinned. Tellingly, their sin made them hide from God. It introduced alienation, suspicion, enmity where before there had only been love, trust, and delight. And nor is it all one way. Our sin has made us justly the objects of God's wrath. Until it has been dealt with we have every reason to be afraid of him.

Then there is our relationship with one another. Few would dream of asking the Bible why it is that we human beings do such a bad job of living together on this planet. Why do we hate, kill, abuse, betray, slander, exploit and steal from one another? But the Bible is the one book that gives us an authoritative answer to that question. Sin! It has not only disrupted our relationship with our Creator. It has put us at odds with one another.

Add to that our mismanagement of the creation. When God made us in his image it was with a view to a great task. Here it is in his own words: 'Let us make man in our image, after our likeness. And let them have dominion over the fish of the sea and over the birds of the heavens and over the livestock and over all the earth and over every creeping thing that creeps on the earth' (Gen. 1:26). God made us lords of his world, custodians of his creation, to take care of it and to harness its resources for the good of humanity and the glory of his name.

Not surprisingly sin has cast its shadow over this too. It has, for example, brought a curse upon the ground – diminishing its fruitfulness and increasing the labour involved in cultivating it for our sustenance (Gen. 3:17, 18). And then, to fill out the picture, think how greedily and recklessly we have exploited the earth's resources, hunted its creatures to extinction, polluted its seas and rivers, poisoned its air, brought ruin on it by our wars, and more. In God's undeserved mercy, there is much we have done successfully and well. But, under the influence of sin, there is much that we have done badly indeed.

What about the future? Why are sickness and ageing ahead for most of us, with death and the grave for us all? Once again, we can give a one-word answer: Sin! The Bible is explicit on that point. 'Sin came into the world through one man [Adam], and death through sin' (Rom. 5:12). Sin has had a devastating impact on our bodies, making them susceptible to disease and death.

Or think how it will be at the end of time. Our sin will bring cataclysmic final judgment on our world. The apostle Peter describes this very graphically in his second letter. The heavens and the earth, he says, are being stored up for fire (2 Pet. 3:7). Immediately after will be the appearing of the entire human race before God's judgment seat. And looming beyond that, 'the eternal fire prepared for the devil and his angels' (Matt. 25:41), which only those who have welcomed God's salvation will escape.

Put all that together and you see how deep and widespread is the damage done by sin. It has ruined everything. And since salvation's purpose is to put everything right, one can appreciate just how many strands there are to it. God has a race to fix and a world to repair. And in fixing the race he must reconcile us to himself, eradicate the effects of sin from our bodies, and so change our hearts and lives that we may live in a proper relationship with him, with one another, and with our world.

A distinct element in the process

It is into this big picture that we fit *sanctification*. It is a distinct element in the process, a major part of the salvation that God is graciously and powerfully bringing about. Specifically, it has do with a change of heart and a change of life – an inward work with an outward result.

Two things that are said about the heart in the Bible – one in the Old Testament and one in the New – soberingly illustrate how great a need there is for such a change. Through the prophet Jeremiah the Lord declares the heart to be 'deceitful above all things and desperately sick' (Jer. 17:9). And then there is this statement from the lips of Jesus: '… from within, out of the heart of man, come evil thoughts, sexual immorality, theft, murder, adultery, coveting, wickedness, deceit, sensuality, envy, slander, pride, foolishness. All these evil things come from within, and they defile a person' (Mark 7:21-23).

Sanctification is the work of God by which these wicked hearts are transformed – and with them our behaviour. It begins, as we shall see, with a deliverance from sin's ruling power (Rom. 6:14), continues on throughout our remaining time on earth, is perfected when we enter heaven, and will be fully lived out in our resurrection bodies in God's new world.

We may illustrate its distinctive features by comparing and contrasting it with another gospel blessing, namely, *justification*. In justification God deals with our guilt; in sanctification with our sinfulness. In justification God puts us right with himself; in sanctification he transforms what we ourselves are and thereby how we live. Justification is a once-for-all event that belongs to the beginning of our Christian experience; sanctification is an ongoing event that lasts the whole of our Christian lives. Justification is perfect and complete from the outset; sanctification is incomplete until we enter heaven.

Sanctification, then, is part of a wider whole, a much bigger picture. The need for it arises from a particular thing that sin has done to us (it has made us sinful). And it consists in a particular thing that God in salvation does for us (he makes us holy). But while sanctification is distinct and must not be confused with the other elements of our salvation, it profoundly affects them. Think of it as colouring the whole – both now and in the future.

Colouring the whole

Take the basic matter of our relationship with God. Through faith in Jesus we are justified. Our sins are pardoned and, through the imputation of Christ's righteousness, our standing with God is completely altered. It is as if we are in a law court and hear the judge pronouncing us not guilty but righteous, and setting us free. But into what kind of life do we then go? How do justified sinners live? They live holy lives. The same Saviour to whom the Spirit has joined us for justification powerfully works in us to make us like himself. Justification and sanctification may be distinct. They are! But they are also inseparable. Those whom God puts right with himself always go on to *live* aright.

Or think about our fellow human beings and how our sanctification affects our relationship with them! It moves us to forgive those who wrong us. It enables us to exhibit what Paul calls 'the fruit of the Spirit': love, joy, peace, patience, kindness, goodness, faithfulness, gentleness, and self-control (Gal. 5:22, 23). And just think how far reaching is the first of these, *love*. 'Love does no wrong to a neighbour' (Rom. 13:10). It prompts us instead to keep those commandments that so profoundly impact our relationships for good – 'You shall not commit adultery; You shall not murder; You shall not steal; You shall not covet' (Rom. 13:9).

Then there are the specifics. Relationships within the family as husbands and wives, parents and children. Relationships within the church as members with members, leaders with those whom they lead. Relationships at work as fellow employees and with people both over us and under us. Relationships in the state as subjects and rulers. Personal relationships, too, both with friends and with enemies. If sin has had a negative impact on all of these relationships (in the case of enemies, actually creating them), sanctification does the opposite. As it changes our hearts and conduct for good it necessarily and powerfully affects them for good too.

Or take the matter of our lordship over the creation. Sanctification touches on that as well. We come to our responsibilities as men and women who now, by grace, love God and want to love our neighbours as ourselves. We are endeavouring to put greed to death, selfishness too. Scripture asserts that one of the marks of a genuinely righteous person is a concern for animal welfare (Prov. 12:10). We sense our accountability to God for his world. All of which is to say that sanctification has a positive impact on the way we care for our planet.

What about our bodies? Sanctification, it must be said, will not deliver them from sickness and death as such. But it will keep us from those diseases that are directly the result of a sinful lifestyle. And it will bring God so very near to us that we will bear our sicknesses with patience and face our end in peace.

Or think ahead to judgment day. The Bible emphatically declares that without holiness 'no one will see the Lord' (Heb. 12:14). How sobering the picture given by our Lord of 'workers of lawlessness' being ordered to depart, forbidden entry to the kingdom of heaven (Matt. 7:21-23)! But on the other hand there are those who will hear *these* words: 'Come, you who are blessed by my Father, inherit the kingdom prepared for you from the foundation of the world' (Matt. 25:34). Who are they? Men and women who have lived holy lives and have shown it by a love for Christ that has manifested itself in a love for his people.

And what an impact sanctification will have on the life of eternity! For we will then be perfect in holiness. We will be living and serving in resurrection bodies and the members of those bodies will only ever be used as instruments for righteousness. Our tongues, our eyes, our ears, our hands, our feet will never serve sin again – only our Saviour. Our joy will at last be full. We will love at last with unsinning heart.

So yes, sanctification is only a part of a larger whole. But it is by no means an incidental part. It is massive in itself. And both is this life and in eternity it colours all the rest.

2

Holy God, Holy People

Y ou are reading your English Bible. It is not apparent, is it, that the words *sanctification* (and its verbal form *sanctify*), *holy* (along with the noun *holiness*), and *saint* all share a common root? But they do, both in New Testament Greek and Old Testament Hebrew. The simplest way to think about how these three words relate to each other is by focusing on the middle word of the three: *holy*. Sanctification is all about being made or becoming holy. A saint is one of God's holy people.

So what is holiness? What does it mean to be a holy man or woman, a saint?

It was stated in the first chapter that it was all to do with a change of heart and life, of character and conduct. To be made holy is to undergo an inward transformation that shows itself outwardly in transformed behaviour. But we need to take a closer look and actually see this truth from God's word.

Separation

We begin with what on the face of it seems a contradiction. Again and again (especially in the Old Testament) the word *holy* is used in connection with separation rather than moral and spiritual transformation. Character and conduct don't come into it. Let us take some examples.

The very first use of the word *holy* is in Exodus 3. Moses, at the burning bush, was told to take off his sandals because the place on which he stood was holy ground (Exod. 3:5). Later in Exodus we have God's words about the Sabbath. It was a day that he had made holy – something that brought with it a corresponding duty of keeping the day holy (20:8, 11). Then there was the tabernacle. It was divided into two parts. The first was called the Holy Place (26:33). Beyond that there was the Most Holy Place (26:34).

Examples could be multiplied. Aaron was to wear holy garments when he officiated as priest (28:4). A holy crown was to be set on his turban (29:6). The oil with which he and his sons were to be anointed was holy (30:25). So too the altar on which he was to offer sacrifices (29:37). There is reference to holy offerings (30:33), holy vessels (2 Chron. 5:5), holy convocations (Lev. 23:3), God's holy hill (Psa. 2:6), and God's holy city (Neh. 11:18).

The fact that all these holy things are inanimate alerts us straight away to something very important. We cannot confine the concept of holiness to the ethical and the spiritual. It is not always about heart and life – hating sin and shunning it, loving righteousness and living it. Holiness is evidently something broader.

So let us ask the question: in what sense could days, garments, places, and offerings be holy? It is here that the word *separation* is helpful. By the will of God all these holy things, mentioned above, were set apart. Separated from other things for special purposes. The Sabbath, for example, was in many respects no different from any other day. The sun rose and set on it exactly as it did on all the other six days of the week. But God had made it different from all the rest by giving it a different function. He had set it apart for special uses and for special activities.

Furthermore, it was God himself who was at the heart of all this holiness. Common things were made holy for his service; for the worship of his name; as an expression of devotion to him; for the purposes of atonement and intercession; that he might dwell in the midst of his people in a way that was safe for them; that he might be honoured and approached aright; that his blessing might be enjoyed; that his wrath might be propitiated and avoided. The holiness of holy things always had to do with people's relationship with God and with his relationship with them.

In this sense God's people themselves were holy. Moses says to God's old covenant people, 'you are a people holy to the Lord your God. The Lord your God has chosen you to be a people for his treasured possession out of all the peoples who are on the face of the earth' (Deut. 7:6). Israel's holiness was not primarily a matter of spiritual transformation and God-honouring life. It had all to do with being separated out from the rest of the nations to be particularly God's people. And when Peter says of

God's new covenant people that they are 'a holy nation, a people for his own possession' (1 Pet. 2:9), the same idea is included. God has set us apart from all the rest of the world for this special function: 'that you may proclaim the excellencies of him who called you out of darkness into his marvellous light' (1 Pet. 2:9).

What about God himself?

There is a remarkable counterpart to this in God himself. He himself is holy. The prophet Isaiah, for example, on almost thirty occasions refers to him as 'the Holy One' or 'the Holy One of Israel.' It is a key part of God's self-revelation in holy Scripture. The God who is, the God who made us, the one living and true God, is *holy*.

There is a decidedly ethical dimension to God's holiness, and we will come to it in moment. But first a question: is there anything corresponding to the separation, the 'set-apartness,' that is central to the concept of holiness as it applies to things and people? In answering that it is helpful to think about the seraphim who cried out in Isaiah's great vision, 'Holy, holy, holy is the LORD of hosts' (Isa. 6:3). What are they saying about him?

One writer answers this in terms of God being 'distinctively other than the realm he has created.'[1] Pantheism denies that. It insists that everything is God. God doesn't merely pervade everything by virtue of his omnipresence. All that exists is God and a manifestation of God.

[1] John L. Mackay, *A Study Commentary on Isaiah, Volume 1: chapters 1-39* (Darlington: Evangelical Press, 2008), p. 163.

Holiness, by contrast, says the exact opposite. There is nothing that is God except God himself. He is *other* than we are. He is separate, belonging to a different order of existence. In himself he is essentially different from all that he has made – ourselves included. He is a being apart from all other beings. In Isaiah's vision this 'apartness' is associated with unrivalled majesty and awesome kingship. 'In the year that King Uzziah died I saw the Lord sitting upon a throne, high and lifted up and the train of his robe filled the temple' (Isa. 6:1). God is in his palace, and he is on his throne, and his throne is high, towering above all earthly thrones, and he has humble and reverent attendants, and he has an army (he is 'the Lord of hosts', Isa. 6:3), and his glory fills the whole earth (6:3). He is also perfectly, dazzlingly, frighteningly, and condemningly *pure*.

I read once of a young man who was living a dissolute life and whose heart was very hard. One day he saw a young woman whom he had known in the past and who had been living a very different kind of life indeed. She was the image of purity and innocence. The sight of her sent him home in anguish, his heart pierced with a sense of his wickedness.

It is something like that which happens to Isaiah. The sight of God in his holiness overwhelms him with a sense of sin. It is as if the holiness of God is a light – a very bright light – and in that light the prophet sees how unclean he is: 'I am a man of unclean lips, and I dwell in the midst of a people of unclean lips' (6:5). The people are polluted, Isaiah shares in that pollution, and the sight of it is devastating: 'Woe is me! For I am lost' (6:5). It seems impossible for a man like him to come so close to the spotlessly holy one and survive.

The holiness of God in us

It is this ethical dimension to the holiness of God that by grace is being reproduced in believers. According to Hebrews 12:10 God disciplines us 'for our good, that we may share in his holiness.' And in Peter's first letter we read the following:

> As obedient children, do not be conformed to the passions of your former ignorance, but as he who has called you is holy, you also be holy in all your conduct, since it is written, 'You shall be holy, for I am holy' (1 Pet. 1:14-16).

We are to be holy too, just like God. Not, of course, in respect of his otherness. We cannot be like him in what distinguishes him from us. But we are to be like him in respect of his purity.

Which brings us back to the idea of *transformation*, to the kind of change in us that we most readily associate with holiness. How can we who are so sinful in our hearts and lives come to resemble our holy God in *his* holiness? That is the very task God has set himself! He will so change us that in heart and in life we become the image of himself – holy as he is holy. There is no sin in him. Sin is the utter contradiction of what he is in his holy heart; it is repugnant to him beyond words. Consequently, in choosing us in Christ to be holy and blameless in his sight (Eph. 1:4), it is the eradication of this sin at which he is

aiming. So, too, the production, in its place, of the purity
with which he shines.

Saints

In the case of every true Christian the work of sanctification
has begun. In the New Testament the Christian believer
is repeatedly called a *saint*. When Paul begins his letter
to the Ephesians by addressing it to 'the saints who are in
Ephesus' (Eph. 1:1), he does not have in mind some special
sub-set of the congregation. He means the believers in
general. According to Romans 1:7 sainthood is one of the
fruits of the call of God; according to Philippians 1:1 it is
one of blessings we possess through our union with Christ.
It belongs to the very definition of a Christian: he or she is
a saint; one of God's holy people.

You do not need to be a miracle worker to be a saint.
In Roman Catholicism sainthood is something officially
conferred by the church but only on certain people – those
who have been very virtuous and to have performed mir-
acles. And if these things are established, and the church
'beatifies' you, you then have special influence in heaven.
People can pray to you and ask you to do things for them.
However, none of this Roman Catholic teaching has any
foundation in the word of God.

Contrary to popular idiom, you do not need to be a
particularly *fine* Christian either. People will say of such
and such a Christian, 'he/she is a real saint.' And they do so
because the believer concerned is so gracious or so patient
or so long-suffering or so generous or so thoughtful of

others. But that also is not how we should think. Saints
are what *all* Christians are – already.

Here, however, is what as a saint you *do* need to be. And
we will be returning to it in a later chapter. You do need to
be holy, in heart and in life; not perfectly, but there must
be grounds for thinking that God has begun a work of
transformation in you. Christians are God's holy people not
just in the sense that he has set them apart for his service
but also in the sense that they are beginning to become like
him in *his* holiness. Holy God, holy people. The question
then is this: Does your life mark you out as one of them?

3

Sanctification: the Work of God

Toward the close of his first letter to the Thessalonians Paul pronounces the following benediction: 'Now may the God of peace sanctify you completely' (1 Thess. 5:23). Our one interest at the moment lies in what this language implies. Sanctification is the work of God. The apostle desires his readers to be perfectly holy and invokes the Lord's power to that end.

We shall see in a later chapter that we ourselves have an all-important role to play. Christians are by no means passive as God does his transforming work in their lives. Sanctification, however, is fundamentally God's work. Even the part that we ourselves play is the product of a prior divine impulse. 'It is God who works in you, both to will and to work for his good pleasure' (Phil. 2:13).

It is to the work of God in making us a holy people that we now turn our attention. In particular, we are going to see that sanctification is a *trinitarian* work. Each of the three persons of the Godhead – Father, Son, and Holy Spirit – has a distinct role to play, although not in isolation from the other two. There is no work that one person does to which the others do not contribute in some way or other. Nevertheless, there is a special activity of the Father, another of the Son, and another of the Holy Spirit.

The activity of the Father

We begin with the special activity of God the Father. It is to him that the Scriptures attribute the *planning* of our sanctification. If we are becoming like him in his holiness it is because from eternity it has been the Father's purpose to make us so. We hear it, for example, in Paul's magnificent introduction to his letter to the Ephesians:

> Blessed be the God and Father of our Lord Jesus Christ, who has blessed us in Christ with every spiritual blessing in the heavenly places, even as he chose us in him before the foundation of the world, that we should be holy and blameless before him (Eph. 1:3, 4).

The presupposition is that God is viewing us in our sin. And his goal in choosing us in Christ is to so change us that we become holy and blameless in his sight.

Paul takes it up again in Romans 8:

> For those whom he [i.e. God the Father] foreknew he also predestined to be conformed to the image of his Son, in order that he might be the firstborn among many brothers (verse 29).

The fall of Adam (and his posterity in him) into sin did not destroy in us the image of God altogether. The fact that we remain divine image-bearers is what makes both the killing and the cursing of our fellow human beings such grave sins (Gen. 9:6; James 3:9). But we did cease to be like God in his holiness. And that in turn determines the Father's goal in salvation. It is to shape us into the likeness of his Son so that he might be the firstborn among a family of brothers who perfectly resemble him in his holiness. As we did at the first.

Let us consider one more text. In his last letter of all, his second letter to Timothy, Paul speaks about

> the power of God, who saved us and called us to [or *with*] a holy calling, not because of our works but because of his own purpose and grace, which he gave us in Christ Jesus before the ages began (2 Tim. 1:9).

The divine calling that comes at the outset of our Christian lives has our holiness as its goal. But why is such a call given? Because by our works we have earned it? On the contrary, the roots of our calling are traced here to a gracious purpose to save us that pre-dates the dawn of time.

The activity of the Son

What about the special activity of God the Son? We begin by going back to Paul's letter to the Ephesians and the purpose of the Father in election. He has chosen us in Christ to be holy (Eph. 1:4). But now comes the big question: how is the Father going to bring this purpose to fruition? Specifically, is he going to proceed as he did when he made the world? Creation, too, was planned out in advance. And in Genesis 1 we are given a vivid picture of the plan being executed. How was it done? With words. 'For he spoke, and it came to be; he commanded, and it stood firm' (Psa. 33:9). What God had purposed was simply willed into being.

When it comes to outworking of the divine plan for salvation, however, it is altogether different. We are certainly intended to trace out parallels between what God did at the beginning and what he is doing in salvation. The fact that creation language is used when speaking of salvation alerts us to that (2 Cor. 5:17; Eph. 4:24). At the point of execution, however, the parallel utterly breaks down. Words are not enough. For God the Father to re-make us in his image nothing less is required than the incarnation and death of the Son of God.

How movingly Paul teaches this in Ephesians 5 when he speaks of Christ loving the church and giving himself up for her,

> that he might sanctify her, having cleansed her by the washing of water by the word, so that he might present the church to himself in splendour, without spot or wrinkle or any such thing, that she might be holy and without blemish (verses 25-27).

Between the eternal plan to make us holy and the fulfilment of that plan in time there is a cross. The special activity of the Son in sanctification is to die for us. In self-giving love he first takes our nature, then suffers in our place that we might be members of his radiantly beautiful, spotlessly holy church.

Furthermore (and we shall be returning to this in a subsequent chapter) it is through our union with Christ in his death that the work of sanctification actually begins. In Romans 6 Paul speaks about our old self being 'crucified with him in order that the body of sin might be brought to nothing, so that we should no longer be enslaved to sin' (verse 6). We are able to walk in newness of life because by grace we have been joined to the Saviour who died for us and rose again on the third day.

The activity of the Holy Spirit

And then we come to the special activity of God the Holy Spirit. It is he who takes the lead, as it were, in the transforming process itself. Peter's first letter, for example, is addressed to 'those who are elect … according to the foreknowledge of God the Father, in the sanctification of the Spirit, for obedience to Jesus Christ and for sprinkling with his blood' (1 Pet. 1:1, 2). The work of setting us apart for God and shaping us into his likeness is declared here to be particularly that of the Spirit. It is he who is at the forefront.

The same truth is evident from the words of Paul that were quoted in the Introduction:

> And we all, with unveiled face, beholding the glory of the Lord, are being transformed into the same image from one degree of glory to another. For this comes from the Lord who is the Spirit (2 Cor. 3:18).

It is through the inner working of the Spirit that we come increasingly to resemble our glorious Lord.

The above are very general statements. But the Scriptures also connect the Spirit with some of the specific aspects of our sanctification – the mortification of sin, for example. In Romans 8 we are warned that if we live according to the flesh we will die, but that if we put to death the deeds (i.e. the misdeeds, the sins) of the body we will live. Nor are we left in any doubt as to how that is to be done: 'by the Spirit' (verse 13).

Then, on the more positive side, it is by the power of the Spirit that we come to produce and to exhibit what Paul terms 'the fruit of the Spirit', namely, 'love, joy, peace, patience, kindness, goodness, faithfulness, gentleness, self-control' (Gal. 5:22, 23). These are common qualities in the sense that each is to be found in the lives of people who are still in the grip of sin. So what makes them distinctively the fruit of the Spirit? He takes each of them and does something special with them – something only he can do by his presence and work in our hearts. Consider love, for instance: in the Spirit's hands love has new objects, springs from new motives, and comes to expression in ways it would never have done before.

It is important to say again that the persons of the Godhead do not operate independently of each other. The Bible affirms both a distinct activity of each and a cooperating of all. It is explicitly said, for instance, that the Father's choice of us to be holy in his sight was made *in Christ* (Eph. 1:4). Christ is at the heart of the divine plan. Then there is Christ's own work. Certainly it was he alone who took our nature and died for us on Calvary. But he was enabled to do this through the Spirit whom the Father had given to him (Heb. 9:14). Similarly with the Spirit himself. It is as the Spirit of the Lord (i.e. the Lord Jesus) that he progressively transforms us (2 Cor. 3:18). Or more generally, the Spirit is at work in new covenant fullness because, in fulfilment of promise, the exalted Jesus received him from the Father and poured him out (Acts 2:33).

Now all that we have just considered alerts us to the greatness, the grandeur of this work. Sanctification is clearly no small matter when each of the three persons of the Godhead individually, and all of them together, are working to make us holy. It takes us indeed to the very heart of what God is doing in saving us from our sins. He is in pursuit of a people who are not only right before his law (justification) but who so resemble him in character that he can have everlasting communion with them.

How enormously humbling it is too! For God to go to all this trouble and to incur such expense and to persevere with it over millennia – isn't that evidence of a quite extraordinary love? How eager must he be to have his image restored and his friendship with us renewed that he is prepared to go to such remarkable lengths to have it so!

Let our commitment to sanctification reflect that. A work which is the fruit of the Father's planning, the Son's suffering and the Spirit's activity in our lives should meet with no half-hearted response from those who are its highly privileged objects. The fervour of God's devotion to making us holy ought always to have its counterpart in the fervour of our devotion to be holy.

4

Looking at Jesus

It is one of the most important questions we can ever ask: is there anything that fundamentally sets us apart as human beings from all the rest of the living creatures on this planet? Evolutionary theory denies it, insisting that we are merely part of a continuum, essentially no different from the lower life forms from which we have evolved. The Bible, by contrast, insists that we *are* different. It also tells us in what way: 'Then God said, "Let us make man in our image, after our likeness" … So God created man in his own image; in the image of God he created him' (Gen. 1:26, 27). Alone of all the living beings God has made, humans bear his image.

One aspect of that image lies in moral character. God did not make our first parents sinful. Sin was not part of our original make-up. Sin came in afterwards – through the temptation and fall recorded in Genesis 3. Adam and Eve formerly were like God in his holiness. That is why we are to think of sanctification as a restorative work. God is working in us to make us morally like himself once again. You were 'taught in Christ' – these are Paul's words to the believers in Ephesus –

> to put off your old self, which belongs to your former manner of life and is corrupt through deceitful desires, and to be renewed in the spirit of your minds, and to put on the new self, created after *the likeness of God* in true righteousness and holiness (Eph. 4:22-24).

Seeing God in Jesus

Marvellously, the Bible allows us to put a human face to this divine likeness – *Jesus'* face. The glorious Lord into whose image we are being transformed from one degree of glory to another (2 Cor. 3:18) is the Lord Jesus Christ. Those whom God foreknew 'he also predestined to be conformed to the image of his Son' (Rom. 8:29). He is himself 'the image of the invisible God' (Col. 1:15), 'the exact imprint of his nature' (Heb. 1:2), as spotlessly holy as God the Father. And now, in grace, that image, as far as moral character is concerned, is being reproduced in us.

Prior to his incarnation the holiness of God was something of which we had only been given glimpses: in the precepts of his holy law; as he acted in accordance with his holy character; as he dwelt in holiness among his people in the tabernacle and later in the temple; as he made holy men and women of those whom he saved. The picture was always a true one but only ever fragmentary.

And then 'the Word became flesh and dwelt among us' (John 1:14). For the first time since the fall there was a man on earth who perfectly resembled God in holiness and righteousness – God himself, in fact, in our nature. And nor was it just for a short time, catastrophically ending as it did before in the Garden of Eden. Through all the demands of daily life, the pressures of public ministry, Satan's temptations, the hostility of enemies, and the sufferings and death of the cross, Jesus persevered in being God's perfectly holy servant to the very end.

It is to his image that we are being conformed as God brings his eternal purpose of salvation to pass. Christ is not only the very life of our sanctification (as we shall see in the next chapter); he is also its pattern. Looking at him we see what we need to become – what, by grace, we are beginning to become – what one day we will fully become as God brings his work in us to completion.

The fruit of the Spirit

To illustrate this we return to something at which we merely glanced in the previous chapter – the fruit of the Spirit. Paul has been giving the Galatian Christians a list of the 'works of the flesh' – ugly products of our sinful human nature: 'sexual immorality, impurity, sensuality, idolatry, sorcery, enmity, strife, jealousy, fits of anger, rivalries, dissensions, divisions, envy, drunkenness, orgies, and things like these' (Gal. 5:19-21) – indicating, by these last words, that he has only made a selection. His list is by no means exhaustive.

Then, over against these ugly things, he places a whole series of beautiful things. He calls them 'the fruit of the Spirit.' They are the very things the Spirit is living in our hearts to produce; their presence in our lives the evidence of his own presence and work – 'love, joy, peace, patience, kindness, goodness, faithfulness, gentleness, self-control' (Gal. 5:22-24).

We noted in the last chapter what makes these distinctively the Spirit's fruit. He takes things that are common to human beings, even in their fallenness, and does something special with them. Love, for example, is common to both believers and unbelievers. But only the believer loves God and out of love obeys him. Only the believer loves believers – loves them *as* believers – and out of love serves them.

It is a very useful exercise to go through the whole list and ponder what each of the nine becomes in the Spirit's hands. Be encouraged to take the time to do it! For now we simply note what we ourselves become as the Spirit produces this fruit in us: increasingly like our Lord Jesus. In *his* love, *his* joy, *his* peace, *his* patience, *his* kindness, *his* goodness, *his* faithfulness, *his* gentleness, and *his* self-control.

The Spirit's ministry in Jesus

As we think about Christ himself exhibiting the Spirit's fruit we begin with the theological foundation. How is God going to save us from our sins? By the instrumentality of the very nature in which we sinned and fell. Ruin came through a man, through his disobedience. And the plan of God is that recovery will come through another man, through his obedience (Rom. 5:19). Hence the incarnation of the eternal Son. He takes our humanity so that in it and through it he might live and die for our salvation.

It is because Jesus was truly human that we can speak about the fruit of the Spirit in his life. How is he is going to live his human life, the divine Son in our nature? Not by drawing upon the resources of his own Godhead but by the aid of the Holy Spirit. Right from the very beginning there is going to be a very special ministry of the Holy Spirit in his life as a man.

The Old Testament announced it in advance: 'The Spirit of the LORD will rest on him – the Spirit of wisdom and understanding, the Spirit of counsel and of power, the Spirit of knowledge and of the fear of the LORD – and he will delight in the fear of the LORD' (Isa. 11:2, 3). It is a prophecy of the coming Messiah. What would he be like? A man on whom the Spirit would rest. And here is how it would be seen: in his wisdom, understanding, counsel, power and, most amazingly of all, in his fear of the Lord. All that he would be as a man of God would be traceable to the ministry of the Spirit.

We hear it, too, in the announcement of the angel to his mother Mary: 'The Holy Spirit will come upon you, and the power of the Most High will overshadow you; therefore the child to be born will be called *holy*' (Luke 1:35). The perfect holiness of Jesus' human nature is to be traced to the presence and ministry of the Holy Spirit. And in the nine-fold fruit of the Spirit, that presence and ministry made itself visible.

Jesus and us

There are two points of contrast with ourselves. The first is that Jesus exhibited *all* of the fruit of the Spirit. It is sobering to realize that until the Spirit comes to indwell and restore us we exhibit *none* of the Spirit's fruit. We have noted already how all nine of the qualities listed can be found in people from whose hearts the Spirit is absent. But it is also the case that in every instance the love, joy, peace, patience, kindness etc. lack what makes them distinctively the fruit of the *Spirit*. Sinners love – but they do not love God. They have joy – but it is not the joy of the Lord. They can be at peace – but it is not 'the peace of God which surpasses all understanding' (Phil. 4:7). Apart from the Spirit's presence and ministry in grace people do not exhibit *any* of the Spirit's fruit.

In the case of Jesus we find the exact opposite. If we by nature lack all of the fruit of the Spirit, he *exhibits* all. The Spirit who created and indwelt his human nature so shaped and enriched it that nothing was missing. The love that only he can produce, the joy that flows from his gracious influence upon the heart, the peace of God himself – these and all the rest are conspicuous in his human life. It is another most useful exercise to go through the Gospel records and trace each of them out. Be encouraged to take the time to do it! And as you do so, say to yourself, it is in order to produce these in me that the Spirit is in my heart too.

And then a second point of contrast. Jesus exhibited the fruit of the Spirit to *perfection*. What do we find when we look for the Spirit's fruit in our own lives? The answer is, an unevenness in the way in which it presents itself. A Christian, for example, may be singularly loving and yet a prey to anxiety, knowing far less of the peace of God in his heart than he ought. Another may be very joyful but not very patient. Christians can be exceedingly kind and yet weak in the area of self-control; unswervingly faithful yet far, at times, from being gentle.

There is no such unevenness in the Saviour. No one characteristic stood out, as it were, beyond the others. He was not strong in one area but not so strong in another. There is a beautiful all-roundedness or symmetry about his life as a man of God. He was *all* of these things: loving, joyful, patient, kind, good, faithful, gentle, and self-controlled; a man whose heart was filled with the peace of God. And at every stage of life he was so to perfection, as a boy, as a youth, as a man.

That is not to say that there was no progression; no growth. We may think of the Spirit taking Jesus' journey through the various stages of life, the curriculum of suffering God ordained for him, his victories in the face of temptation, his experiences of men and God, and using them to bring about a maturing, a deepening, a widening of all his graces of character. He was, after all, truly human. But there was never anything lacking. Nothing was ever marred by sin. He never had to repent of any of the shortcomings over which we ourselves have continually to lament.

Which in turn is what makes him our model; our pattern for holy living. It is why the Spirit is working in us to conform us to his likeness. It is why as we bear more of the Spirit's fruit we become increasingly like him. It is why when the Spirit has finished his work in us we will be *perfectly* like Jesus. He himself exhibited *all* of the fruit of the Spirit, and did so to *perfection*.

5

How It All Begins

S anctification isn't done in a day. It is in fact a life-long
process and in subsequent chapters we will be looking
at the biblical evidence for that. The beginning of our Christian lives is only the beginning of the work of transforming
us into the likeness of Christ. There is a long and difficult
journey ahead.

It is also true, however, that the beginning in question is
a *big* beginning. If there is anything in our world that gets
off to a great start it is the process of making us holy. And
this quite independent of the lifestyle that has preceded
it. The change in a Saul of Tarsus, by his own confession
'a blasphemer, persecutor and insolent opponent' (1 Tim.
1:13), was patently revolutionary. But it is no less so in a
little girl of ten who has grown up in a Christian home, has
been obedient to her parents, and has been largely shielded
from the evil of the world. For her, too, the inward change
when she first comes to Christ is massive.

The very way in which the word *sanctified* is used in
the New Testament is a pointer to this. Paul addresses the

believers in Corinth, for example, as 'those sanctified in Christ Jesus, called to be saints' (1 Cor. 1:2). It had already happened! In Christ Jesus they had been sanctified. Later on, referring back to the change that had taken place in their lives, he says, 'And such were some of you. But you were washed, you were sanctified, you were justified in the name of the Lord Jesus Christ and by the Spirit of our God' (1 Cor. 6:11). Sanctification is presented as a blessing already theirs.

There is a parallel here with being called by God, born again, justified, and adopted. Each of these is a once-for-all event occurring at the start of the Christian life. So too is being sanctified. This is not to deny that sanctification is ongoing. But it does alert us to the magnitude of what happens at the outset. This great event has been called *definitive* sanctification (in contrast to *progressive* sanctification). Or the distinction may be put like this: Christians are not only *becoming* holy; they are *already* holy. It is this initial transformation, and just how far reaching it is in every case, that forms the subject of the present chapter.

In no part of Scripture is clearer light shed on it than in Romans chapter 6. In previous chapters of his letter to the Romans Paul has been focusing on God in salvation putting us right with himself, sorting out our relationship with him. Now, in chapter 6, he moves on to how God in salvation gets to work *in* us, making us different from what we were. And here is what he tells us: in becoming Christians we experience nothing less than a death and resurrection. We naturally think of these as future things. There is an important sense, however, in which for the believer they have happened already. We have died and risen to life again. 'It is to be part of your Christian self-consciousness,' says Paul: 'So you must also consider yourselves dead to sin and alive to God in Christ Jesus' (Rom. 6:11).

The death that we died

In Romans 6:6 Paul makes reference to 'our old self.' He means by that phrase the person we were when we were separate from Christ. How was it with us then? We were slaves! 'Our old self was crucified with Christ in order that the body of sin might be brought to nothing, so that we would no longer be enslaved to sin.' Later in the chapter he takes it up again. In verse 17 he asserts that his readers were 'once slaves of sin'; in verse 19 that they had once presented their members 'as slaves to impurity and to lawlessness leading to more lawlessness.' He is thinking about sin as *power* – a controlling power, an enslaving power. It is why we lived the sinful lives we did, why with our bodies we said and did the sinful things that we did. Sin had us in its grip. It had our bodies in its grip. It wasn't Jesus who was our lord. It was our sinful selves.

But now things have changed!

> But thanks be to God, that you who were once slaves of sin have become obedient from the heart to the standard of teaching to which you were committed, and, having been set free from sin, have become slaves of righteousness (Rom. 6:17, 18).

We are no longer our old selves! Sin is no longer the enslaving power that it once was: 'you have been set free from sin and have become slaves of God' (Rom. 6:22). Our lives are now being shaped and determined by *him*. And here is how it happened: there was a death. We 'died to sin' (Rom. 6:2). Our old self was crucified with Christ (Rom. 6:6).

In order to understand this we need to bring Christ himself into the picture. Romans presents him to us as the perfect and complete answer to the problems our sin has created – sin as *guilt*, for example. Jesus is the answer to that. Our first father Adam has entailed sin, condemnation, and death on all his descendants, but when by faith we come to be united to Christ the fatal link is broken. In and through him we enjoy instead the counter blessings of righteousness, justification, and life. That is the teaching of Romans 5. And now in Romans 6, we see deliverance from sin as *power*. For those who by faith are united to Christ there is freedom from sin as an enslaving power and grace to live a new life.

It is to this union that Paul refers when he speaks about being 'crucified with him' (Rom. 6:6). So too in his earlier words: 'Do you not know that all of us who were baptised into Christ Jesus were baptised into his death? We were therefore buried with him through baptism into death' (verses 3, 4). It is the amazing thing that is symbolized in baptism – death and burial with Christ. And resurrection too – as we shall see.

As we puzzle over this it is all-important to remember that it is *Jesus* to whom we are joined: Jesus the *victor*, the one who by his death has done all that is necessary to deliver us from both the guilt and power of sin. He comes into our lives as a man on a mission, a search-and-destroy mission. He is *after* something: our old sin-dominated life; sin as an enslaving power. He gets it in his sights and goes for it. And he doesn't miss. He strikes it a deadly blow and down it comes, toppled from its throne. He says to sin, 'You shall not bear rule in this heart any longer!' And that's the end of sin's domination. Because of the death Jesus himself died to sin (Rom. 6:10) we die to sin as well. Lordship is wrested from sin's hands and passes into the hands of Jesus.

The resurrection that followed

Which brings us to the remarkable sequel. If there is a death at the outset of our Christian lives there is also a resurrection. Union with the Jesus who died and rose to life again gives us both. This too is symbolized in baptism: 'We were buried with him by baptism into death, in order that, just as Christ was raised from the dead by the glory of the Father, we too might walk in newness of life' (Rom. 6:4). Or again, 'For if we have been united with him in a death like his, we shall certainly be united with him in a resurrection like his' (verse 5). The one is as certain as the other. Just as death was followed by resurrection for him, so for those who are one with him.

We may think, by way of illustration, of the death and resurrection that are ahead for us. What will they do? They will take us out of one realm and bring us into another. Death will take us out of a world that has been stained and ruined by sin. Resurrection will bring us into another world in which everything has been made new. Similarly with the death and resurrection that are past. It means passing from one realm into another, out of a realm in which sin holds sway to one where God holds sway. And it happens through our union with Jesus in his death and resurrection. In and through him we too begin to walk in newness of life.

In the second half of Romans 6, Paul spells out how this dramatic change is to show itself. As God's freed people there are things that we *are* to do and there are things that we are *not* to do.

What we are *not* to do is summed up in Romans 6:12, 13: 'Let not sin therefore reign in your mortal body, to make you obey its passions. Do not present your members to sin as instruments for unrighteousness.' You understand what that language implies. Sin itself has not been annihilated. It is still an active power in the believer's life. I can well imagine Christians wrestling with this language of death and resurrection – dying to sin and rising in Christ – and wondering if it has really happened, fearing that perhaps it has not. They know that sin is alive and strong. They are conscious of it every day. Every time they pray they have to confess that it has, in this way or that, got the better of them. Then they come to Romans 6, hear what union with Christ has done, and wonder if it can possibly be true for them.

That is why we must be careful not to push the language of death and resurrection beyond what it is intended to teach. What has ended is not sin's existence but sin's domination. What Christ has put to death is not sin itself but the life in which it dominated. Because of him it is no longer an enslaving power. That is why we can now live a life that is pleasing to God. Nevertheless, sin itself remains – a tempting, troubling, tripping-up power, ever seeking to regain its old mastery. It wants its throne back! And Paul says, 'Don't let it take control! Don't give it what it wants. Don't put the parts of your body at its disposal. It wants to use your eyes, your tongue, your limbs, your brain for its own wicked ends. Resist it!'

But he does not leave it there. He moves on to the positive:

> Do not present your members to sin as instruments for unrighteousness, *but* present yourselves to God as those who have been brought from death to life, and your members to God as instruments for righteousness (verse 13).

Or again,

> just as you once presented your members as slaves to impurity and to lawlessness, so now present your members as slaves to righteousness leading to sanctification (verse 19).

The parts of our body are to be put at the disposal of righteousness, of God. Or here is how Paul puts it later in Romans:

> I appeal to you therefore, brothers, by the mercies of God, to present your bodies as a living sacrifice, holy and acceptable to God, which is your spiritual worship (12:1).

We are to live as servants of the one who is now our rightful Master. Ourselves as a whole and all our parts are *his* and are to be used by him in his service as instruments for righteousness, for the good of others, for his glory and their salvation. That is the call of God on our lives. It was once impossible to live such a life; as impossible as it is for a slave to live as a free man or woman. But not any longer. Through union with Christ we have been freed from sin's dominion. And by virtue of that same union we can live every day as a freed man or woman ought.

6

Plain Sailing?

God has been at work in your life, drawing you to his Son. Because of that you may think of yourself as sanctified. You are now one of God's holy people! Your faith in Christ has brought you into a union with him that has so freed you from the controlling influence of sin that you both can and do live the God-pleasing life it was once impossible for you to live.

We now begin to look at what is ahead. For the new Christian has by no means 'arrived.' Sanctification may have got off to a great start (it has!) but it is certainly not complete. It is the journey, rather, of a lifetime. The reason for that can be summed up very simply: sin is still present and at work in the believer's heart and life. We noted in the previous chapter (and it is an all-important distinction), that what ends when faith unites us to Christ is sin's domination, not its existence. Sin itself remains in us and is strong and busy. Sanctification, as a consequence, is a progressive thing. As we set ourselves to the task of dealing with our sin and growing in grace we become, by God's blessing, *increasingly* holy, more and more like Jesus.

The object of this chapter is to demonstrate from Scripture what believers know from experience, namely, that progressive sanctification is anything but plain sailing. It is a struggle, a fight, an unrelentingly arduous work. Remaining sin was described a few pages back as a tempting, troubling, tripping-up power, ever seeking to regain its old mastery. Imagine a cruel dictator who has been replaced by a ruler who is wise and just and kind. Great! But the dictator isn't dead. Nor has he accepted the new order. On the contrary he is ceaselessly at work to try and get back what he has lost. So with the sin which the Lord has toppled from its throne. It wants to be what it was before – in charge. And not until the end of our days will it give up the attempt. The result? Conflict!

The apostle Paul touches on this in the fifth chapter of his letter to the Galatians. He is contrasting the desires of the flesh (our still-so-sinful nature) and the desires of the Spirit (who has graciously come to live in us to make us holy), and says that 'the desires of the flesh are against the Spirit, and the desires of the Spirit are against the flesh, for these are opposed to each other, to keep you from doing the things you want to do' (verse 17). We are conscious of being pulled in two different directions – by the Spirit toward what is good, by the flesh toward what is evil. And the outcome is not always a happy one. When Paul writes at the end of the verse about being kept from doing what we want to do, it is likely that he is thinking about indwelling sin carrying the day, preventing us from doing what in our Spirit-renewed hearts we would much prefer to do.

Christianity, therefore, is by no means conflict-free. Nor is this a mere matter of maturity, as if in time we might outgrow it. Paul himself is proof of that. The most moving account of this inner conflict is from his own pen in Romans 7:14-25. Writing about himself as an experienced believer, Paul opens a window for us on just how difficult is the life of holiness.

It needs to be said by way of preface that we are in a conflict-zone just as *readers* of Romans 7. That is because there is disagreement as to what the apostle is actually doing in these verses. Specifically, is he really describing what life is like for him as a Christian? Some deny that, arguing that what he is giving us here is a picture of how things were before he came to Christ. And certainly there are statements which seem to lend colour to that argument. Some important lines of evidence, however, have persuaded a majority of expositors in the Reformed tradition that he is writing of himself as a *Christian*. It will be helpful to glance at them and then draw out some conclusions for ourselves.

The evidence

Paul's *grammar*. And lest any should experience a sinking of heart at the thought of an argument from grammar, let me quickly assure them that the point in question is a simple one! It has all to do with a change of tense. The section of Romans 7 immediately preceding (verses 7-23) is also autobiographical. As in the later section, verses

14-25, Paul is writing about himself. And he does so using the *past* tense. He is looking back to his unconverted days and telling us how the sin of covetousness shattered his self-righteousness: 'sin, seizing an opportunity through the commandment, produced in me all kinds of covetousness' (verse 8). Or again, 'sin, seizing an opportunity through the commandment, deceived me and through it killed me' (verse 11).

When Paul moves into the later section the tense changes. He is no longer writing about the past but rather about the present. For example, 'I do not do what I want, but I do the very thing I hate' (verse 15). Or again, 'I have the desire to do what is right, but not the ability to carry it out' (verse 18). Or again, 'I find it to be a law that when I want to do right, evil lies close at hand' (verse 21). Or once more, 'Wretched man that I *am*!' (verse 24). Paul is describing his present experience; the conflict with sin that is his as he pens his letter to the Romans.

Paul's *emotions*. Reference is made in this section to two entirely opposite emotions: delight and disgust. On the one hand, in verse 22, Paul confesses that in his inner being he delights in the law of God. On the other hand, the sin into which he is so often betrayed is clearly detestable to him. It is, he says, 'the very thing I hate' (verse 15). Both are pointers to a renewed heart. It is the Christlike man who loathes wickedness (Heb. 1:9); the blessed man who takes delight in God's law (Psa. 1).

Paul's *mind*. Right at the end of chapter 7 Paul says, 'I myself serve the law of God with my *mind*' (verse 25). In

44

order to appreciate the significance of this we have to make a little excursion into Romans 8 and notice what is said about the mind there. In Romans 8:7 Paul speaks about how 'the mind that is set on the flesh is hostile to God, for it does not submit to God's law; indeed, it cannot.' It is a description of what Paul himself was once like when the authority of the tenth commandment was so fiercely resisted. But it is not where he is as he writes his letter to the Romans. With his mind now, i.e. with what is deepest in his personality, he *serves* the law of God. He is its willing servant, eager to do what it commands.

Paul's *will*. If we were to ask Paul what was most basic in terms of his heart's desire, what he wanted more than anything to be able to do, here is what his answer would be: to do the will of God. To sin was to do the very thing that he did not want to do; it was to act contrary to his deepest wishes. The whole bent of Paul's will was toward the doing of God's will. Jesus could say that he always did those things that were pleasing to the Father (John 8:29). The man of Romans 7 wishes he could say the same. How do we account for that? Only by the transformation of which Paul has been writing in the previous chapter, Romans 6.

Conclusions

Paul, then, is writing as a Christian – as a mature and indeed eminent Christian. And it enables us to draw the following conclusions about the life of holiness into which union with Christ has brought us. What may we expect to find as we move on from that initial encounter with Jesus that has so radically changed us? The following:

Imperfection. The message of Romans 6 is that we are not what we once were: 'having been set free from sin,' we 'have become slaves of righteousness' (6:18). It is also the message of Romans 7. In the opening section Paul speaks about believers having 'died to the law' (7:4). What does he mean by that? In the days before we came to know the Lord his law stood 'outside' us as it were, directing us, condemning us, stirring up our hearts (through no fault of its own) to disobedience, deepening our bondage to sin and to guilt. But now, through our union with Christ, all has changed. God's law is now the will of the one whom we love. It is our delight. We are now able (7:4) to live fruitful lives of obedience to it, and do.

So we are not what we once were! But we have not yet been made perfect. That is clearly implied in what Paul says in Romans 6 about not letting sin reign in our mortal bodies; about refusing to present our members to sin as instruments for unrighteousness (6:12, 13). And it is writ large over the final section of Romans 7. Why is it that we so often find ourselves where Paul was, wanting to do good and yet doing instead the very thing that we hate? We have not yet been made perfect. Sin is still in our hearts.

Conflict. The sin that remains in us is neither weak nor asleep. It no longer holds sway as Christ has sovereignly dethroned it. But it is still powerful and active, never giving up the effort to exercise the dominion it did in the past. Hence the inner war with which every Christian is familiar. As often as we want to do good, evil is right there with us to oppose us (7:21). The heart of the Christian is a battleground. Do not conclude that, because you find this conflict in yourself, that you are either a very poor Christian or perhaps not a Christian at all. On the contrary, it is normal Christianity. The desire and effort to do what is pleasing to the Lord never go unopposed.

Sorrow. How is the war proceeding? Are we always victorious, unfailingly successful in resisting temptation, and in winning the day against indwelling sin, and never giving in? If only! Our experience is exactly like Paul's. We delight in God's law in our inner being and with our minds we serve it. Our lives are fundamentally characterized by a glad obedience to our Saviour. But sin is so strong and we are so weak that many times we do give in; we do the very thing that we hate. And it is a grief to us. We feel Paul's pain as he cries out 'wretched man that I am!' (7:24) and know that pain ourselves. Sorrow! It is by no means our whole experience. But there is no escaping it. We want to please the one who has set us free. And when we don't, it pierces our hearts.

So is it plain sailing, then, as our chapter heading asks? Anything but! Sanctification launches us upon a life of imperfection, conflict, and sorrow. Don't be surprised, therefore, when you find it so. At the same time, we must not let the severity of the struggle obscure the glory of our hope. Having cried out, 'Wretched man that I am! Who will deliver me from this body of death?' (7:24), Paul immediately exclaims, 'Thanks be to God through Jesus

Christ our Lord!' (7:25). When Christ returns and makes all things new the imperfection, the conflict and the sorrow will be forever at an end. Our hope in Christ is a hope of deliverance. And it is a sure hope. That is why we can join the apostle in giving thanks. He who has begun a good work in us will carry it on to completion until the day of Christ Jesus (Phil. 1:6).

7

Time To Get the Knife Out

The Lord has risen from the dead and is about to return to heaven. Before he does so he gives an important charge to his disciples. It is known as the Great Commission and is recorded for us by Matthew in the closing verses of his Gospel. We may think of it as Jesus' programme for the church until his return:

> Go … and make disciples of all nations, baptising them in the name of the Father and of the Son and of the Holy Spirit, teaching them to observe all that I have commanded you' (Matt. 28:16-20).

It is the last part that gives us the lead-in to our present chapter. The Great Commission is not fulfilled merely by the making and the baptising of disciples. Those disciples are also to be taught. Specifically, taught to live lives of *obedience*.

It was how Christ himself lived. We learn from Hebrews 10:7 that David's words in Psalm 40 were prophetically Christ's own words: 'Behold, I have come to do your will, O God.' As Paul puts it in Galatians 4, he was 'born of woman, born under the law' (verse 4), shouldering humanity's responsibility to live a life of obedience to God. And he did it perfectly. Speaking of his Father in heaven he could say, 'I always do the things that are pleasing to him' (John 8:29). Here, too, is what he said to his disciples on the eve of his death: 'If you keep my commandments, you will abide in my love, just as I have kept my Father's commandments and abide in his love' (John 15:10). Nor did he set limits to it, refusing to go the whole of the painful distance ordained for him. On the contrary, 'he humbled himself by becoming obedient to the point of death, even death on a cross' (Phil. 2:8).

We are to think of this obedience as the basis for our justification. Contrasting Adam with Christ, Paul writes that 'as by the one man's [Adam's] disobedience the many were made sinners, so by the one man's [Christ's] obedience the many will be made righteous' (Rom. 5:19). Just as Adam by his sin put us in the wrong with God, Jesus by his obedience puts us right with him. When we believe in Christ for salvation his obedience is put down to our account. It is reckoned ours. And on the basis of it, God forgives our sins and accepts us as righteous in his sight.

But Christ's obedience is also the model of our sanctification. What does a holy life look like? What does it actually mean to live a holy life? Look at Jesus Christ! As he lived, so also are we to live. As obedience marked him, so obedience is to mark us. It is our duty to ascertain from the whole of Scripture what is the will of God for us and, in the strength of the Spirit, to live in conformity to it just as Christ did. Nor is this obedience a matter of mere outward conformity. Speaking through David, Christ could say, 'I *delight* to do your will, O my God; your law is within my heart' (Psa. 40:8). Exactly the same is true of us if grace has made us one with Christ. God's law is within our hearts too. We too delight to do his will. And the more that is so, the holier our lives.

Back to the struggle

If we are ever to live like this, however, we must address the problem of remaining sin. Sin, as we have seen, is still alive and active in our hearts and wanting its former place of lordship back. When Paul says to us, 'Let not sin … reign in your mortal body, to make you obey its passions' (Rom. 6:12), he is making its desires and objectives crystal clear. It is eager to have its own way again and we must not yield to it. Otherwise a holy, obedient, Christ-like life will be impossible. Hence Paul's plea that we do not let sin reign in us as it once did. Hence his insistence that instead of presenting the members of our bodies to sin as instruments for unrighteousness, we present them to God as instruments for righteousness (6.13). We are to put ourselves at *his* disposal, not at *sin's*.

A little later in Romans Paul takes up the subject of our conflict with sin again, this time from a different angle. He writes,

> So then, brothers, we are debtors, not to the flesh, to live according to the flesh. For if you live according to the flesh

you will die, but if by the Spirit you put to death the deeds
of the body you will live (Rom. 8:12, 13).

The translation of *deeds* as *misdeeds* in one modern Bible
version is interpretive rather than literal. But it captures
the meaning exactly. Sin manifests itself in the misdeeds
of the body, in the things we say and do when sin gets
control of us. And Paul's directive is that we wage war
against these misdeeds and that it be a war to the death. It
is what Christians have in mind when they speak about the
mortification of sin. To this all-important topic we devote
the remainder of this chapter.

In using the language of *killing* Paul is telling us in a
very graphic way that we must deal with our sins ruthlessly.
They are to be given no quarter. It must be our unrelenting
aim to rid our lives of them. But how is that to be done?
The Bible answers that question in at least the following
two ways:

By saying 'no' to them. We are being tempted to sin.
Sin is appealing to us to let it have its way. What does the
Bible continually tell us to do in those circumstances? To
say 'no.' To refuse to let sin have its way. We have heard
that already from Romans 6. God's word categorically pro-
hibits us from letting sin reign in our bodies. We are not
to obey its passions. We are not to put our bodily parts at
its disposal. And then the Bible goes into detail. It names
specific sins to which we are vulnerable and orders us to
abstain from them. Here are some examples from Paul's
letter to the Ephesians:

> Let the thief no longer steal ... Let no corrupting talk
> come out of your mouths ... Let all bitterness and wrath
> and anger and clamour and slander be put away from you
> ... But sexual immorality and all impurity or covetousness
> must not even be named among you ... (4:28, 29, 31; 5:3).

It is an unquestionably effective way of ridding our lives
of sinful deeds. Say 'no' to them.

By steering clear of them. Jesus has the following stern
words for his disciples:

> And if your hand or foot causes you to sin, cut it off and
> throw it away. It is better for you to enter life crippled or
> lame than with two hands or two feet to be thrown into
> the eternal fire. And if your eye causes you to sin, tear it
> out and throw it away. It is better for you to enter life with
> one eye than with two eyes to be thrown into the hell of
> fire (Matt. 18:8, 9).

Our Lord is not calling us to literally dismember ourselves. His concern is with the things that cause us to sin
and with the importance of cutting them out of our lives,
even when that is costly or painful. It has its application to
our computers, our companions, to the places we go, the
magazines we read, the things we watch on television. If
something is drawing us into sin it must go. That way we
steer clear of sin.

Now obviously this is no easy task and that for several
reasons. One is the *time* factor. When Paul speaks in
Romans 8 about putting to death the misdeeds of the body
he is using the present continuous tense. This is something

we go on doing. Every day that we live we must say 'no' to sin and endeavour to steer clear of it. There is no let up. Add to that the *attractiveness* factor. One of the surest proofs that our hearts are still sinful is that sin is still desirable. Our duty is to say 'no' when we would rather say 'yes;' to steer clear of sin when we would rather indulge it. How easy the task of mortifying sin if sin had no attraction for us! And then there is the *pain* factor. Jesus may not be calling us to literally cut off hands and pluck out eyes. But if his language means anything there is pain involved in living a holy life. The cutting off of a friendship, for example, may be necessary because it is spiritually harmful to us. Waging war against sin is tough.

The help of the Spirit

Paul reminds us, however, that God has done more than lay on us this arduous duty. He has also given us help. It is, he says, 'by the Spirit' that we put to death the misdeeds of the body (Rom. 8:13). The mortification of sin is not something that we are to attempt in our own strength but by the aid of the Spirit. It is one of the great reasons why God has given him to us. He has come as the Spirit of Christ to enable us to refuse sin's lordship and live under Christ's lordship instead.

It is to the Spirit, for example, that we trace the change of heart that is at the root of all holy living. We have been thinking about the life that Jesus lived, a life of obedience to God. That obedience was the fruit of what he was inwardly. Specifically, it evidenced his love of righteousness and hatred of wickedness (Heb. 1:9). In a similar way the Spirit helps us. He is at work in us to make our hearts like that of Jesus. Through his transforming ministry we too come to love righteousness and hate wickedness. And under the impulse of these powerful affections we are able to say *No* to sin and to steer clear of it.

Again, there are his promptings: to pray; to read and meditate on the Scriptures; to unite with God's people for worship on the Lord's Day; to sit under the preaching of God's word; to make conscience of coming to the Lord's table. And then as we *heed* his promptings there is the blessing he makes these things to be to us. We have this difficult task of mortifying sin and we ourselves are so weak. But through the things to which he prompts us the strength that we need is continually given. It impresses on us our indebtedness to the Spirit. So too the importance of not grieving or resisting him but cultivating a close relationship with him.

Motives

We close this chapter by glancing at the motives Paul gives for heeding his counsel. One of these is the warning about death: 'if you live according to the flesh you will die' (Rom. 8:13). Paul is looking at what lies at the end of the road. 'Let sin reign in your mortal body,' he is saying; 'let it have its way and live as it desires and you will not see heaven.' It is something on which the New Testament is insistent. No holiness, no heaven (Heb. 12:14). 'Not everyone who says to me, "Lord, Lord," will enter the kingdom of heaven, but

the one who does the will of my Father who is in heaven'
(Matt. 7:21).

And then there is the promise of life: 'If by the Spirit
you put to death the [mis]deeds of the body, you will live'
(Rom. 8:13). The apostle is looking again at what lies at
the end of the road. This time, life! If we are believers we
have it at present. And if we persevere in our battle with
sin it will one day be ours in all its fullness. Everlastingly!
In other words, the Bible never allows us to imagine that
our warfare with sin isn't worthwhile. On the contrary, it
is more than worthwhile. We have everything to lose if we
give up and let sin have its way, and everything to gain if,
with the Spirit's help, we sustain the warfare to the end.

8

Expectations

L ife is full of finished projects. You have some piece
of work to do, you make a start, you work at it, and
eventually, after hours or weeks or months or years, it is
done. Can it ever be like that with sanctification? I am not
thinking here about dying and passing into glory. When
that happens our sanctification most certainly will be
complete. My question has rather to do with *this* life. How
high can we pitch our expectations as we think about the
shorter or longer period that lies between the present and
the end of our lives?

Let us change the image and tie the question in with
what we have been looking at in previous chapters. Sanctification gets off to a great start. Sin is dislodged from the
throne of our lives and compelled to give way to Christ. But
it is not yet dead. Nor is it dormant. It remains a powerful
and active force in us. War is therefore unavoidable. Sin
is fighting back and if it is not to get the better of us we
must deal with it ruthlessly. May we hope, however, for

final victory before the end? Can sin be eradicated short of death? Or if not eradicated, is it possible to attain to such a degree of sanctification that we are able to live sin-free or conflict-free Christian lives?

There are Christians who have unhesitatingly answered *yes*. Some, for example, have taught a work of the Holy Spirit so powerful that it leaves the soul 'perfect in love and as pure as unfallen Adam.'[1] The writer just quoted recalls an aged lady who told how for forty years she had been kept from sin in thought, word, and deed. Her heart, she declared, 'was no longer "deceitful above all things, and desperately wicked," but was as holy as the courts of heaven, since the blood of Christ had washed away the last remains of inbred sin.'[2]

Others, whilst denying that sin has been taken out of our hearts, have nevertheless insisted that it is possible to live without sinning. Contemporary English theologian, J. I. Packer, writes of those who 'while rejecting sinlessness of heart … proclaimed sinlessness of acts in the sense of deliverance from all known wrong,' depicting the Christian life 'as potentially one of total and endless victory over every form of temptation and moral weakness.'[3]

It is important to stress that none who hold the above views would say that we are ever out of danger. What has been attained can easily be lost. But they would unite in

[1] H. A. Ironside, *Holiness The False and The True* (New York: Loizeaux Brothers, nd) p. 15.

[2] Ironside, *Holiness The False and The True*, p. 16.

[3] J. I. Packer, *Keep in Step with the Spirit* (sec. ed., Leicester: Inter-Varsity Press, 1990), p. 148.

saying that the kind of conflict with sin and defeat by sin and sorrow over sin with which most Christians are only too familiar need not continue until the Lord takes us to heaven.

Remaining sin

In responding to these claims we begin with the presence of sin itself in our hearts and lives. Scripture holds out no expectation whatsoever that God will take sin out of us this side of the grave. The letter to the Hebrews does speak about 'the spirits of the righteous made perfect' (Heb. 12:23). But it clearly locates them in heaven. Deliverance from indwelling sin is what they enjoy *now*. For as long as they were alive on the earth they had to carry it with them. As we do.

It may be helpful at this point to remind ourselves that salvation is a line rather than a point. It is said that a Christian scholar of a previous generation was once accosted by a young woman anxious to know if he was saved. His reply was to the following effect: 'It depends on the tense of the verb you are using. Do you mean, "Have I been saved? Am I being saved? Or am I yet to be saved?"' All three are true of us if we are Christians. We have *been* saved, we are *being* saved, and we are yet *to be* saved. Salvation does not come in its fullness in a once-for-all experience. It is an ongoing experience with a beginning, an end, and a long in-between.

How does it begin? With the regenerating work of the Spirit; with the call of God the Father; with faith in Christ;

with repentance of sin; with the blessings of justification and adoption; with definitive sanctification. In all these senses we have been *saved*. Then there are the future aspects. Paul in Romans 13 speaks about our salvation 'being nearer now than when we first believed' (Rom. 13:11). Peter, in his first letter, speaks about 'a salvation ready to be revealed in the last time' (1 Pet. 1:5). It is not God's will to exempt us from death *now* or to give us a new body *now*. These are blessings for which we wait. They belong to the *not yet* of salvation experience. So too deliverance from indwelling sin. Like our fall-affected bodies it will travel with us to the end.

To suppose, therefore, that sin can be eradicated before the end is a serious mistake. To imagine that it has *been* eradicated is a delusion. Hebrews speaks about 'the deceitfulness of sin' (Heb. 3:13). Don't let it deceive you into thinking it has gone! It has not, regardless of how far advanced you may be in your sanctification. The believer who truly knows himself *disclaims* perfection – as Paul did (Phil. 3:12).

Our adversary the devil

A second thing we can expect is the relentless activity of our adversary the devil. It is not true to say that all temptation comes from him. James asserts that 'each person is tempted when he is lured and enticed by his own desire' (James 1:14). Many of our temptations arise from within our own sinful hearts. But they also come from outside; directly from the devil. They are among the 'the flaming arrows of the evil one' of which Paul speaks in his famous passage on spiritual warfare (Eph. 6:16). And there is no promise of exemption from them.

The sixteenth-century Scottish Reformer John Knox tells of how one such arrow was fired at him on his death-bed. Awaking from an evidently troubled sleep and being asked the explanation he replied,

> I have formerly, during my frail life, sustained many contests, and many assaults of Satan; but at present he hath assailed me most fearfully, and put forth all his strength to devour and make an end of me at once. Often before has he placed my sins before my eyes, often tempted me to despair, often endeavoured to ensnare me by the allurements of the world; but these weapons were broken by the sword of the Spirit, the word of God, and the enemy failed. Now he has attacked me in another way; the cunning serpent has laboured to persuade me that I have merited heaven and eternal blessedness by the faithful discharge of my ministry. But blessed be God, who has enabled me to beat down and quench this fiery dart, by suggesting to me such passages of Scripture as these – 'What hast thou that thou hast not received? – By the grace of God I am what I am – Not I, but the grace of God in me.' Upon this, as one vanquished, he left me.[1]

Right to the end of our lives he is our hate-filled enemy and will take whatever opportunities he is granted to assault us. And not just with temptations of his own making. He

---

[1] Thomas M'Crie, *Life of John Knox* (Ter-Centenary Edition, Edinburgh and London: William Blackwood and Sons, 1884), p.276.

will take the desires of our sinful hearts and urge us to give free rein to them. And he will take the sinful things of the world and use them to stir up lust or fear. We may expect no let up. He will remain a threat to the holy lives we have been called to live until the very end.

The world

One further thing we can expect has to do with the world just mentioned; the world in which we are living out our lives. We do know that one day it will be totally transformed. 'According to his promise we are waiting for new heavens and a new earth in which righteousness dwells' (2 Pet. 3:13). But until our Lord Jesus returns it will remain essentially as it is. God may bless us again with revivals on the scale of the sixteenth-century Reformation or the Great Awakening of the eighteenth century. But it will remain an ungodly world till the close. Our fallen human race will continue in rebellion against its Maker and will continue to manifest that in its thinking, its laws, its practices, its religions, its literature, and its leisure pursuits. The context in which we are called to live out holy lives is therefore a very difficult one. The world would have us conform to its ungodly standards, and exerts relentless pressure to make us do so.

It is the combination of these three things – remaining sin, a busy devil, and an evil world – which compels us to pitch our expectations considerably lower than some Christians would do. Prior to heaven there can be no sinlessness of heart because it is the will of God that our natures remain fallen until then. And prior to heaven there can be no sinlessness of life because indwelling sin, our enemy the devil, and this ungodly world, both singly and together, make such a life impossible. Had God in his word held out to us the possibility of such grace being ours as to lift us above these influences, this chapter would come to a very different conclusion. But no such grace is promised. There is no secret to be discovered that provides us with the key; no dramatic life-changing experience that puts us above the conflict. The teachings of Romans 6, 7, and 8 that have been before us in previous chapters constitute the norm for the Christian life until its earthly phase is over.

None of this is to deny that extraordinary progress can be made. Provided we stop short of perfection we may say that the Christian's potential for growth is limitless. It is to our shame that we are not holier Christians than we are. We may please God more and more (1 Thess. 4:1). We may bear more and more of the fruit of the Spirit. The process by which we are transformed into the Lord's image from one degree of glory to another (2 Cor. 3:18) may and should continue as long as life itself lasts. In a word, we may become ever increasingly like Jesus – inwardly and outwardly, in heart and in life – and should make it our life-long ambition to be so.

But we are to be realistic. Great harm has been done by holding out expectations that are unrealistic. Some have imagined a perfection that was not true of them and it has made them proud and censorious. Others have felt only too keenly how far they have fallen short, for all their earnest seeking; and it has led to disillusionment, to depression, even to madness, and, sometimes, to a rejection of Christianity altogether.

We shall give the last word to John Newton, author of the hymn 'Amazing Grace,' and prince of letter-writers. Writing of how the 'distressing effects of the remnants of indwelling sin are overruled for good,' he says:

> By these experiences the believer is weaned more from self, and taught more highly to prize and more absolutely to rely on him, who is appointed to us of God, Wisdom, Righteousness, Sanctification, and Redemption ... Again, a sense of these evils will (when hardly anything else can do it) reconcile us to the thought of death; yea, make us desirous to depart that we may sin no more, since we find depravity so deep-rooted in our nature, that (like the leprous house) the whole fabric must be taken down before we can be freed from its defilement. Then, and not till then, we shall be able to do the thing that we would: when we see Jesus, we shall be transformed into his image, and have done with sin and sorrow for ever.[1]

---

[1] John Newton, *Select Letters of John Newton* (Edinburgh: Banner of Truth Trust, 2011), pp. 144-5.

9

The All-Important Setting

My knowledge of plants and trees is shamefully slight but I know enough to be aware of the importance of the setting. Living things are dependent for their health and growth on factors such as soil, sunlight, moisture, air, and temperature. These constitute the 'setting' within which their life develops and fruitfulness takes place.

It is no different with the believer's sanctification. There is a setting within which we grow in our likeness to Jesus Christ. Just as plants and trees need the right soil and the right amounts of light and rainfall, so there are factors on which we are equally dependent if we are to become increasingly holy. Or to put it another way, God works through *means*. There are things that he uses to bring us on; to make us more fruitful. Our object in this chapter and the next is to examine a number of these.

God's word
The first is *God's word*. This bears on our sanctification in a whole range of different ways. We go back, for example,

to the very beginning of the Christian life. The Spirit of God works in us to bring us to faith in Jesus and thereby into transforming union with him. How does he do that? Through the hearing and understanding of the gospel. The word of God, in the Spirit's hands, powerfully initiates the life of holiness.

Then there is Christ our pattern. God's predestinating purpose is to conform us to the image of his Son. We know that because the word of God tells us so (Rom. 8:29). Nor does that word leave us wondering what the image of God's Son is. On the contrary, in the four Gospels – Matthew, Mark, Luke, and John – God's Son is set before us in all his beauty and perfection. As we see him living in costly obedience to the Father and exhibiting the fruit of the Spirit we come face to face with all the respects in which we are to resemble him. There is no uncertainty as to God's goal in working to make us holy. Just look at Jesus.

What about the perils? The broader setting in which we live out our Christian life is that of a world that is hostile to God and under the sway of the evil one. There are dangers on every hand; so much that is inimical to a life of godliness. How plainly the word of God teaches that! And in how many different ways it alerts us, warns us, puts us on our guard, points us in the right direction. It is a lamp to our feet and a light to our path (Psa. 119:105), just exactly the book we need as we make our way to heaven through a dark and dangerous world.

Or take the law of God. A sinful life is a life in which the law of God is disregarded and violated; a holy life is one in which that law is loved and obeyed. But where do we go to find this law? To God's word. And not just to the New Testament. God uses the whole of his word, from Genesis to Revelation, to teach us what we are to believe about himself and how he wishes us to live.

In connection with God's law there is the ministry of the Spirit in convicting us of sin and bringing us to repentance. That ministry is not only ours at the outset of the Christian life (as we see from the narrative of the Day of Pentecost in Acts) but continues all the way through. As Christians sadly we sin. But God in his mercy doesn't leave us in our sin. Through his word and by the Spirit he shows us our transgression and brings us to repentance. The classic biblical example of that is King David (2 Sam. 12; Psa. 51).

Some specific Scripture verses also come to mind. Peter, for example, in his first letter speaks about believers having purified their souls by their 'obedience to the truth' (1 Pet. 1:22), and later urges them 'like newborn infants' to 'long for the pure spiritual milk,' so that by it they might 'grow up into salvation' (2:2). Or take the prayer of our Lord Jesus that the Father would sanctify us through the truth, adding, 'your word is truth' (John 17:17). God makes us the believers he has set us apart to be by his 'word of truth' (Eph. 1:13; Col. 1:5) Or think of Paul in Romans 12:2, appealing to us not to be conformed to this world but to be transformed through the renewing of our minds. How does such renewal take place? Only as our thinking is shaped by the truth of the word of God.

We see from all of this (and there is so much more that could be added) how central is God's word to our sanctification. If we would grow in grace we must be committedly a people of the *Book* – reading it, meditating on it, delighting in it, listening to it taught and preached (of which more in the next chapter), and obeying it. It is God's powerful instrument for making us holy. Let no one live in neglect of it!

Prayer

From the Bible we turn secondly to *prayer*. And as with the Bible and sanctification so with prayer and sanctification: the two connect in a number of different ways. Take, to begin with, the Bible's picture of a holy man or woman. What do we see when we look at it? Certainly obedience to God's law. But so also prayerfulness. It is one of the initial evidences that God has been at work in saving power, Saul of Tarsus being a case in point. Ananias of Damascus is instructed to 'go to the street called Straight, and at the house of Judas look for a man of Tarsus called Saul, for behold, he is praying' (Acts 9:11). Nor do we *stop* praying. Christianity is fundamentally a restored relationship with the God from whom sin has separated us. How bizarre if he only ever spoke to us and we never spoke to him! But it doesn't happen like that. Whatever struggles Christians may have in the area of prayer they do pray. It is another respect in which God by the Spirit conforms us to the likeness of his Son. In his humanity *he* prayed. So also do his people.

Let us be more specific. We may find in our prayers the evidence or otherwise that we are maturing as Christians; becoming less selfish; growing more like our Saviour. The prayer that he himself taught us – the Lord's Prayer – serves that precise purpose. We all know how it begins: 'Our Father in heaven, hallowed be your name. Your kingdom come, your will be done, on earth as it is in heaven' (Matt. 6:9-10). These opening petitions establish priorities for prayer. What are the main things for which we should be asking as we come before the Lord? The hallowing of God's name, the coming of his kingdom, the doing of his will on earth as it is in done in heaven. We need not insist on these coming first in every prayer we offer, either individually or corporately. But we may judge our spiritual progress by the extent to which our prayers as a whole reflect these priorities. Sin has made us selfish. It is a sign of our as yet imperfect sanctification that our selfishness manifests itself in our prayers, making us preoccupied with matters that touch most immediately on ourselves and our loved ones. To be able to break free of that and be taken up with these infinitely bigger things is a sign of growth in grace.

Then there is prayer for sanctification itself. We have an example of this in Psalm 51 in connection with repentance and restoration. The sorrowing David, returning to the Lord from his great sin, prays, 'Create in me a clean heart, O God, and renew a right spirit within me' (Psa. 51:10). Later his plea is, 'Restore to me the joy of your salvation, and uphold me with a willing spirit' (verse 12). Remember, too, the fourth Beatitude: 'Blessed are those who hunger and thirst for righteousness, for they shall be filled' (Matt. 5:4). How does that hunger come to expression? One way for sure is in prayer for righteousness. And God in fulfilment of his promise answers by giving us the very thing sought.

Suffering

The way in which God sometimes answers such prayers gives us our lead-in to a third and final point: how God makes sanctification happen *through suffering*. No better illustration can be given than in the hymn by John Newton, 'Prayer Answered by Crosses':

> I ask'd the Lord that I might grow
> In faith, and love, and every grace;
> Might more of His salvation know,
> And seek more earnestly His face.
>
> 'Twas He who taught me thus to pray,
> And He, I trust, has answer'd prayer
> But it has been in such a way
> As almost drove me to despair.
>
> I hop'd that in some favour'd hour
> At once he'd answer my request;
> And by His love's constraining power,
> Subdue my sins and give me rest.
>
> Instead of this, He made me feel
> The hidden evils of my heart;
> And let the angry powers of hell
> Assault my soul in every part.

> Yea, more, with His own hand He seem'd
> Intent to aggravate my woe;
> Cross'd all the fair designs I schem'd,
> Blasted my gourds, and laid me low.
>
> 'Lord, why is this?' I trembling cried:
> 'Wilt Thou pursue Thy worm to death?'
> ''Tis in this way,' the Lord replied,
> 'I answer prayer for grace and faith.
>
> 'These inward trials I employ,
> From self and pride to set thee free;
> And break thy schemes of earthly joy,
> That thou may'st seek thy all in Me.'[1]

To say that God *always* answers in this way would not be true. God has other, gentler, less painful ways of granting us the holiness for which we plead. The happiness of marriage, for example, or the joy of parenthood. But it is unquestionably *one* of his ways, as Christians in every age have proved.

But we need to come to Scripture itself. Think, for example, of the words of Jesus in John 15:

> I am the true vine, and my Father is the vinedresser. Every branch in me that does not bear fruit he takes away, and every branch that does bear fruit he prunes, that it may bear more fruit (John 15:1, 2).

The image of the pruning knife speaks only too plainly of greater fruitfulness coming through suffering.

[1] 'Prayer Answered by Crosses,' *Olney Hymns, Works of John Newton* (Edinburgh: Banner of Truth Trust, 2015), vol. 2, p. 729.

Or take Paul's words in Romans 5: We 'rejoice in our sufferings,' he says. And here is why: 'knowing that suffering produces endurance, and endurance produces character, and character produces hope' (Rom. 5:3, 4). We become the persevering Christians God wants, Christians of tested and approved character, as God brings us through a curriculum of suffering.

One aspect of this suffering has to do with chastisement or discipline. The letter to the Hebrews assures us that God

> disciplines us for our good, that we may share in his holiness. For the moment all discipline seems painful rather than pleasant, but later it yields the peaceful fruit of righteousness to those who have been trained by it (Heb. 12:10, 11).

These words remind us of something most important. Suffering does not sanctify us automatically. In and of itself suffering can embitter and harden. But in the hands of the Holy Spirit it is unquestionably one of the Lord's primary means for changing us into his likeness. As it casts us upon the Lord, as it brings us to repentance, as it gives us tender hearts toward fellow sufferers, as it draws the Lord near to us in sympathy and with strength, we come, by his grace, to be more and more the Christians he would have us to be. All of which makes suffering among our best blessings.

10

Not in Isolation

Three thousand people converted on the Day of Pentecost through the preaching of one sermon. Imagine! What a demonstration of the power of the Holy Spirit to convict people of sin and bring them to repentance! Of especial interest is the way Luke sums up the result: 'So those who received his [Peter's] word were baptised, and there were added that day about three thousand souls' (Acts 2:41). Added to what? To the infant New Testament church. Conversion not only put them right with the Jesus whom they had so wickedly killed; it also brought them into membership of his church.

In the following verse we see how this membership came to practical expression: 'And they devoted themselves to the apostles' teaching and the fellowship, to the breaking of bread and the prayers' (2:42). The focus is on *togetherness*. These early Christians did not live out their new life in Christ in isolation from one another. They were continually coming together; doing things together

– listening to teaching, sharing what they had with those in need, breaking bread, praying. They were a *body*. That is the image that is repeatedly used in the New Testament when it speaks of the church (Rom. 12:5; 1 Cor. 12:27; Eph. 1:23; Col. 1:18). And evidently after Pentecost these believers were *functioning* as a body.

This present chapter is a continuation of the previous one. Do you remember its theme? The all-important setting within which we grow in our likeness to Jesus; the things that God uses to bring us on; to make us more fruitful; how he works through means. We considered three of them: God's word, prayer, and suffering. And now we come to a fourth: the *church*. In our pursuit of holiness we are not intended to go it alone. God brings us to greater maturity in Christ in the context of our participation in the life of the church.

Teaching and listening

We have been reflecting at some length on the place of Holy Scripture in our sanctification and there is no need to go over the details again. The one thing that needs to be added to the picture, however, is the way in which we use Scripture. How do we so engage with it that it becomes the instrument of sanctification God means it to be? One way, unquestionably, is through our personal reading. Since there was necessarily little of that in the days of the apostles when copies of God's word were bulky, rare, and expensive, how these early believers would have envied us had they foreseen how astonishingly accessible is the word of God to us! Shame on us if, with all our amazing privileges, the Bible is little read!

But if they could not be great readers they could be great listeners. And they were! Acts tells us that 'they *devoted* themselves to the apostles' teaching' (2:42). There was a commitment on the part of the apostles to teaching them God's word that was fully matched by the new Christians' enthusiasm for listening to it. The pattern is for our imitation. There are admittedly no longer any apostles. But Christ has given us pastors and teachers to expound and apply to us his word (Eph. 4:11ff.). He has also given us the Lord's Day and other times to meet with the church. Be encouraged to take the fullest advantage of these opportunities so that in the company of your fellow Christians you might continually be learning and growing.

The Lord's Supper

We learn from Acts 2 that another of the things to which the early believers devoted themselves was 'the breaking of bread' (2:42). There is some difference of opinion as to whether Luke is referring in these words to the Lord's Supper. My own judgment, and it's a common one, is that he is. What is not disputed is that the Lord's Supper was an important part of early church life. So it has continued to the present. On the eve of his death the Lord Jesus commanded his disciples to eat and drink in remembrance of him. And though the church's thinking and practice with regard to this ordinance has often been seriously adrift from Scripture, she has faithfully continued to observe it.

It is one of the most basic facts of Christian life that obedience brings blessing. Psalm 19 says of God's commands that 'in keeping them there is great reward' (Psa. 19:11). Obedience to the command to come to the Lord's table is a case in point. It ought to be said that we come to the Lord's table more in the character of givers than receivers. The Lord's Supper is a memorial feast at which we commemorate a Saviour who loved us and gave himself for us. We are first of all there to celebrate his goodness, to give thanks to him, and to proclaim his death. But in giving we unquestionably receive. So generations of Christians have found it. The Lord who instituted the Supper continues to be present, presiding as he did at the first Supper, and enriching us as we come to him in faith, eager for his blessing.

In what ways? Here is one writer's answer:

> If we ask, 'What ... do we get at the Lord's table?' the best analysis I know is given indirectly in the Shorter Catechism, in reply to the question, 'What are the benefits which in this life do accompany or flow from justification, adoption, and sanctification?' (Question 36). The answer is: 'Assurance of God's love, peace of conscience, joy in the Holy Ghost, increase [or growth] of grace, and perseverance therein to the end.' That's an excellent summary of the feast awaiting us at the Lord's Supper![1]

That being so, let me exhort you to come with your fellow Christians to the Lord's table as often as you are free to do

[1] Donald Macleod, *A Faith to Live By, Understanding Christian Doctrine* (sec. ed., Tain, Ross-shire: Christian Focus Publications, 2010), p. 258.

so. First of all for Christ's own sake, but so also for your own.

Church discipline

There may be comparatively few churches that practise it but church discipline, where there is a need for it, is clearly a biblical duty. I am thinking here specifically about what we might call *exclusionary* church discipline. In his first letter to the Corinthians Paul says,

> I am writing to you not to associate with anyone who bears the name of brother if he is guilty of sexual immorality or greedy, or is an idolater, reviler, drunkard, or swindler – not even to eat with such a one (1 Cor. 5:11).

In his second letter to the Thessalonians the apostle gives an identical directive: 'If anyone does not obey what we say in this letter, take note of that person, and have nothing to do with him, that he may be ashamed' (2 Thess. 3:14). In both letters believers are commanded to dissociate themselves from particular individuals because of their sin.

What does that mean in practical terms? The original Greek word that Paul uses in both letters has the idea of not mixing ourselves up with someone. There is to be a withdrawing from them, an excluding of them. The church is, as it were, to draw a circle around itself and into that circle the one sinning is no longer to be admitted. What does *that* mean? At the very least – and on this there is universal agreement – it means exclusion from the Lord's table. The sinning one has been free to sit down with the church fellowship at the Lord's table, but not any longer; not until there is repentance. Which brings us to the *goal* of such discipline.

It can seem such an unloving thing to do, which is perhaps why it is so widely neglected. But the reverse is in the fact the case. Undoubtedly church discipline can be practised unlovingly. But it is in itself a loving act for its goal is the offender's repentance and restoration. We see this in 2 Thessalonians 3:14, for example. There is to be a dissociation from the one sinning so 'that he may be ashamed' of his conduct and put matters right. The object in view is his amendment.

We see the same in 1 Corinthians 5. Here the discipline is evidently more severe. It involves the same refusal to associate with the one in the wrong. But it goes beyond that. The Thessalonian offenders are still to be treated as brothers (2 Thess. 3:15). Not the man of 1 Corinthians 5. He is to be regarded and treated as an evildoer. Handed over to Satan. His whole connection with the church is to cease. Perhaps he was prohibited from even meeting with the church. The goal, however, was still his repentance and restoration: 'so that his spirit may be saved in the day of the Lord' (1 Cor. 5:5).

It is of course best not to sin at all. That goes without saying. But what a blessing it is if we do fall into sin to be part of a church that takes church discipline seriously. For church discipline is one of the Lord's instruments of sanctification. Through his people he takes action to restore us to himself. If anyone reading these words has been placed under such discipline, let it do its intended work. Let it bring you to repentance and to walking with God again.

Mutual care and ministry

In each of the above the elders of the church have a key role to play, teaching the word of God, administering the Lord's Supper, taking the lead in church discipline. But it is not just the elders who make the church a setting for sanctification. Church members in general do the same as they engage in mutual care and ministry.

A helpful starting place is Hebrews 10:24, 25:

> Let us consider how to stir up one another to love and good works, not neglecting to meet together, as is the habit of some, but encouraging one another, and all the more as you see the Day approaching.

One of the great ends for which we come together as a church is to exhort or encourage one another, something that is all the more important the closer we get to the day of Jesus' return.

So how do we do it? One way – and this may come as a surprise – is through our singing. For according to Ephesians 5:19, in psalms and hymns and spiritual songs believers address one another. Again, to the Colossians Paul writes, 'Let the word of Christ dwell in you richly, teaching and admonishing one another in all wisdom' (Col. 3:16). Similarly in 1 Thessalonians 5:14, he says, 'And we urge you, brothers, admonish the idle, encourage the fainthearted, help the weak, be patient with them all.' What is being envisaged in all of these texts is mutual care and ministry. Believers are not only to take their own holiness seriously but that of their fellow believers too. Both in the meetings themselves and in our conversations before and afterwards we are to consciously aim at what will help our fellow Christians to persevere and grow in grace.

Summary

Much more could be said. But we have seen enough to establish the point: sanctification is not intended by God to happen in isolation. And though the focus of this chapter has been exclusively on the outworking of that in the church it would be easy to expand it to include society as a whole. It was a grave error when men and women abandoned normal family life and interaction with their neighbours and retreated into caves and convents and monasteries. The result was not greater holiness but less. God's contexts for making saintly people are social: the family, the world, the church.

11

Blessings along the Way

I am wondering if it is strictly true to say that I love climbing a hill. Given how painful and tiring the ascent often is, it is perhaps more accurate to say that I love reaching the summit. I tell myself, when my body is breathless and aching, 'it will be worth it when you get there.' And I assure you it always is, even when the view is limited to a few yards (a not infrequent occurrence on Scottish hills!).

It is a bit like that with sanctification. To live a holy life is no easy thing. We have seen that repeatedly in the course of this book. Indwelling sin is ever seeking to hinder us, resisting it often involves painful choices, and one of God's means of making us more like Jesus is suffering. What will help to keep us going? One thing, the chief thing, is where our journey will end. God is going to carry on his work in us until we arrive in his presence perfect. And Scripture assures us that in God's presence is 'fullness of joy' (Psa. 16:11).

But what about the here and now, as we continue on? Are the blessings of sanctification all in the future? By no means! Every lover of the hills will tell you that reaching the top is certainly not the only pleasure. The clean air, the solitude, the ever-changing views, the glimpses of the wildlife, a clearly marked path, and a pair of good boots, all have their part to play as well. So with sanctification. There are blessings along the way as well as at the end. In this chapter we will explore a few of them.

Holiness and happiness

The first is *joy* or *happiness* (I am using the two words interchangeably). We have just been hearing from Psalm 16 that there is fullness of joy in the presence of God. Why is heaven such a *happy* place? One big reason is that heaven is a *holy* place. God is holy, his angels are holy, and so too all his people there. Sin is totally absent. Now sin is the parent of all misery and suffering. Our world was a happy place until Adam and Eve rebelled against God. Holiness meant happiness. It does so in God's case. One great reason why God is called in Scripture 'the blessed God' (1 Tim. 1:11) is because he is perfectly holy. And holiness meant happiness for Adam and Eve too.

But all that changed when they sinned. Read through Genesis 3 and you will see it. Whether it's the fig leaves, or their hiding from God, or the blame-shifting, or the prospect of suffering and death, or their ejection from the Garden of Eden, there is just no missing it: sin robbed them of their joy. And it has been doing the same to their descendants ever since. All the sadness with which this world is so full is ultimately to be traced to sin.

That in turn gives us an important perspective on salvation. It is the road back to happiness. To be delivered from sin is to be delivered from the world's great joy-destroyer. And one day the deliverance will be complete. When God rids the world of sin and makes all things new our joy will once again be full. In the meantime we have foretastes. Forgiveness brings joy. Sanctification does too. Christians who determinedly shun sin and walk in holiness find great happiness in doing so; just as those who compromise with the world and grieve the Holy Spirit inevitably do so at the expense of their joy. Bishop J. C. Ryle, author of a classic nineteenth-century book on holiness, sums it up like this:

> No doubt there are some Christians who from ill-health, or family trials, or other secret causes, enjoy little sensible comfort, and go mourning all their days on the way to heaven. But these are exceptional cases. As a general rule, in the long run of life, it will be found that 'sanctified' people are the happiest people on earth. They have solid comforts which the world can neither give nor take away.[1]

Holiness and beauty

A second blessing is *beauty*. If there is the closest relationship between holiness and happiness, so too between holiness and beauty. Nowhere do we see this more clearly than in the life and character of our Lord Jesus. For those who have the God-given capacity to estimate him truly, there is no one lovelier than he. Jesus is the perfection of

[1] J. C. Ryle, *Holiness* (second enlarged ed.; Edinburgh: Banner of Truth Trust, 2014), p. 44.

all moral and spiritual beauty. We see it in his relationship with his Father in heaven, whom he pleased in every way. We see it as well in his relationship with people, so loving, so selfless, so gentle, so just.

That being so, a growing beauty is the inevitable fruit of a growing holiness in ourselves. For the purpose of God in sanctification is to conform us to the image of his Son (Rom. 8:29). The more we become like him, therefore, the more of his beauty we exhibit. Who are the loveliest Christians of all? Those who most resemble their Saviour: who love with a love like his, rejoice with a joy like his, trust God with a faith like his, hate ungodliness with a hatred like his, and sympathize with a sympathy like his.

Primarily, of course, this beauty shows itself in our character and actions. But it may also be seen in our very faces. 'Many old faces,' says one writer,

> have hard lines, grim angles, cold and cruel aspects. They reflect what the man has become in his soul. They are the faces of men who are self-centred, unloving, and unhelpful.[1]

By contrast there are faces that in their sweetness, gentleness, peace, and radiance reflect a heart and life long and deeply devoted to Christ. Believers cannot see it by looking at themselves in the mirror. But others may see it, perhaps in contrast with the face of someone far from God.

---

[1] W. M. Clow, *The Secret of the Lord* (2nd ed.; London: Hodder and Stoughton, 1911), p. 188.

Holiness and usefulness

A third blessing of holiness is *usefulness*. Place it, to begin with, against the dark background of the harm done to individuals, to congregations, and to the cause of Christ in the world by the sins of professing Christians: inconsistencies in the lives of Christian parents, for example; the divisiveness of a church member; the sharp practices of a Christian businessman; the fall into sin of a pastor. God alone can measure the damage such things do. If sin is the destroyer of our happiness it is no less the destroyer of our usefulness.

Holiness, by contrast, is one of the great keys to Christian usefulness. We see it in our Lord Jesus Christ. He was the Lord's servant, here to do God's will, having as his goal the accomplishing of a world's salvation. How was he able to successfully carry it through? By his unwavering obedience (Rom. 5:19). He always did those things that pleased his Father (John 8:29). He is a Saviour to all who call on him and an example to all his followers because of the holy man that he was and the holy life that he lived.

Holiness is the key to *our* usefulness too. Bishop Ryle puts it so well:

> I believe that far more is done for Christ's kingdom by the holy living of believers than we are at all aware of. There is a reality about such living which makes men feel, and obliges them to think. It carries a weight and influence with it which nothing else can give. It makes religion beautiful, and draws men to consider it, like a lighthouse seen afar off.[1]

[1] Ryle, *Holiness*, p. 58.

Therefore if we would be truly useful members of Christ's kingdom let us give ourselves to the ardent pursuit of holiness. Our obedient lives, our love and joy and peace, our prayerfulness, our compassion, our zeal for the gospel, and our thankfulness will make us powerful instruments in the hand of God for good to our children, to our fellow citizens to whom we are called to be light, to our Christian brothers and sisters.

Holiness and assurance

It is the clear teaching of Paul in Romans 8 that one of the things the Holy Spirit does in the lives of believers is give them assurance of their salvation. In Romans 8:14, for example, Paul states, 'For all who are led by the Spirit of God are sons of God.' In the following verse he speaks about having 'received the Spirit of adoption as sons, by whom we cry, "Abba! Father!"' (verse 15). Then in verse 16 he says that 'the Spirit himself bears witness with our spirit that we are children of God.' In saving us God has brought us into his family. We are his adopted sons and daughters. And the job of the Holy Spirit is to assure us of that fact so that in our hearts we can have the comfort and the joy of it.

But here is the question: how does the Spirit do this? A helpful starting point is the leading of the Spirit to which Paul refers in Romans 8:14. What does it mean to be led by the Spirit? It means to be living, by his grace, under his lordship or leadership. It has all to do with the Spirit shaping and directing how we think and speak and act and worship. If this is what he is doing in our lives it is a sign that we are truly the children of God. Notice, too, the very first word of Romans 8:14: *for*. It links verse 14 with the previous verse where Paul has been speaking about putting to death, by the Spirit, the deeds or misdeeds of the body. Are you following the Spirit's leading in regard to *that*? Seeking in his strength to deal with remaining sin? It is an evidence of being truly a child of God.

Let us bring in the emphasis of Romans 8.16, the Spirit bearing witness with our spirits that we are children of God. We may think about it in terms of the Spirit opening our eyes to what he is doing in our hearts and lives, enabling us, for example, to put sin to death. We *see* what he is doing and it strengthens our conviction that God has indeed become our Father. Holiness, in other words, is at the heart of the Spirit's ministry of assurance. It is the Christian who is serious about dealing with his sin and walking with God who will ordinarily (there are exceptions) have the blessing of *knowing* that he belongs to God's family.

Holiness and God's glory

Romans warns us that 'those who are in the flesh cannot please God' (Rom. 8:8). Until God begins transforming us it is impossible to give him pleasure and bring him glory. After the work has begun, however, it is altogether different. The Thessalonian Christians were walking so as 'to please God' and Paul's exhortation was that they 'do so more and more' (1 Thess. 4:1). Then he gets down to specifics: 'For this is the will of God, your sanctification; that you abstain from sexual immorality; that each one of you know how to control his own body in holiness and honour' (verses 3, 4). How do we live God-pleasing, God-honouring, God-glorifying lives? By living *sanctified* lives. Lives, in other words, that are sexually pure. And beyond that, lives characterized by obedience to everything else that God requires.

Take it as another incentive to press on. View it as another blessing along the way, bound up with all the rest and crowning the whole. There was a time when such a life was utterly (and shamefully) beyond us. Now, by God's grace, we can both delight him and bring him praise, more and more.

12

Reality Check

Y ou have heard of such people. Perhaps you know some of them. Perhaps you are one of them yourself. They profess to be Christians. They are sure that they *are* Christians. But there is unquestionably something missing. A big thing. *Holiness*. They are not living as Christians ought. They will admit that themselves. There are glaring sins in their lives. Or secret sins. Or both. And they are not being dealt with as sins ought. Repentance isn't happening. It is only their beliefs that separate them from those who make no Christian profession at all. At the level of lifestyle they are practically indistinguishable. Indeed there are plenty of non-Christians who are far more honest, or sexually pure, or truthful, or kind, or content, or moderate in their use of alcohol than they are.

Let us ask a question. It will take us right to the heart of what this chapter is about: does it matter? And I mean by that, does it matter for *them* that they are living unholy lives, indulging sin rather than putting it to death, behaving like Jesus' enemies rather than like his friends? In the evangelical world at large a two-fold answer to that is often given. Here is how it goes:

First, it *does* matter how Christians live. Those who ignore the teaching of God's word and lapse into a lifestyle in which Christ has no say will not fail to be the losers by it. For one thing, there will be chastisement. In some way or other they will know God's fatherly anger and it will not be pleasant. Nor will the Day of Judgment be pleasant either. They will suffer the loss of the rewards that would otherwise be theirs had they lived a holy life. There may in fact be none at all. In that sense they will, by their unholiness, be *eternally* the losers.

But second, it is *not* a matter of heaven or hell. The way that Christians live does not affect their eternal destiny. If they are believers in Jesus their unholiness will not rob them of heaven. Certainly their sin will cost them. No question about that. No one can live in habitual disregard of the commandments of God without incurring loss. But whatever that loss, it will always fall short of heaven.

Miserable in heaven

To this two-fold answer I want to make a two-fold response. I invite you in the first place to imagine, of all things, being miserable in heaven.

Not everyone, of course, believes in heaven, nor in hell. Either there is no after-life at all or humans are simply absorbed, at death, into the broader life of the universe. For the professing Christians of whom we are thinking, however, heaven is a given. There may be things in the Bible that are not to their liking and impossible to accept, but heaven isn't among them. They sincerely believe that there is such a place. So too that when they die it is where they will go. Certainly, at their funeral, it is where people will say that they have gone, and think them happy there.

Let us suppose now, for argument's sake, that heaven were to open its gates to them this very hour. Their life on earth is suddenly at an end; with equal suddenness they find themselves in heaven. Would they be happy there? Or would they in fact be miserable? I dare say that for believers to imagine themselves miserable in heaven is to imagine the unimaginable. Aren't we told in the Bible that there are no tears in heaven? No death or mourning or crying or pain? We are! What the Bible calls 'the former things' have passed away (Rev. 21:4). God has made everything new. What is all this nonsense, then, about being miserable?

In truth, it is not the nonsense it seems. Suppose, by way of illustration, that every night for the next two months you are required to attend a concert of classical music. If, like me, you are a lover of classical music and the pieces to be heard are all by your favourite composers performed by world-class musicians, you might relish the prospect and, in the event, enjoy every single moment. But what if you loathe classical music? What if your musical tastes are such that to listen, say, to a Beethoven piano concerto, though exquisitely played, is sheer torture? What pleasure can you promise yourself from your sixty upcoming concerts? You are going to be miserable!

With that in mind, let us return to thinking about heaven. There is no question but that its citizens are happy! Even more so when heaven assumes its final form, that of a thoroughly renovated physical world. Everything that the Bible says about the perfect and unending joy of believers is literally true. But here is why they are happy. They have a taste for heaven's pleasures and occupations. They love its inhabitants, its laws, and all the things that make it different from the world as it is at the moment. Supremely they love its God and King and delight in his company.

Do you see why the kind of people described earlier would be miserable in heaven? However orthodox their beliefs may be, God is not the centre of their lives. Spending time with him, talking to him, singing his praise, doing his will, bringing him glory are not their delight. They do not love holiness. They do not hate sin. To be deprived of all possibility of ever indulging in sin has no attraction for them. Nor does the prospect of only ever living with people for whom Jesus is all in all. Heaven for such would be no heaven at all.

Absent from heaven

We need to take things a large step further, however, and insist that the question as to whether the unholy would be happy in heaven or not will never be put to the test. Why? Because the unholy will be absent from heaven. The view that nothing more is at stake here than blessings in this life and rewards in the life to come is a deadly error. What is at stake is *heaven itself*. The Bible could not be plainer:

those who live in habitual disregard of the will of God, God will send to hell.

Let me ask you to ponder very carefully the following passages of Scripture. The first we have already considered in an earlier chapter, Romans 8:13: 'For if you live according to the flesh you will die, but if by the Spirit you put to death the [mis]deeds of the body you will live.' We are face to face with a stark alternative here. There has to be a death. That is unavoidable. The question is, will the death be our own, or will it be our sins'? To live according to flesh is to let sin alone, to allow it to have its way, to refuse to wage against it a war of extermination. It is how many professing Christians are living. God, through Paul, says that if that is how it continues, it will end in our death. And by 'death' he means 'the second death, the lake of fire' (Rev. 20:14).

Here is Paul again, this time in his first letter to the Corinthians:

> … do you not know that the unrighteous will not inherit the kingdom of God? Do not be deceived: neither the sexually immoral, nor idolaters, nor adulterers, nor men who practise homosexuality, nor thieves, nor the greedy, nor drunkards, nor revilers, nor swindlers will inherit the kingdom of God (1 Cor. 6:9, 10).

Isn't it telling that Paul should exhort his readers not to be deceived? Sin is deceitful (Heb. 3:13). It pulls the wool over our eyes, persuading us that we are safe when we are not.

In his letter to the Ephesians Paul strikes exactly the same note:

> But sexual immorality and all impurity or covetousness
> must not even be named among you, as is proper among
> saints. Let there be no filthiness nor foolish talk nor crude
> joking, which are out of place. But instead let there be
> thanksgiving. For you may be sure of this, that everyone
> who is sexually impure, or who is covetous (that is, an
> idolater), has no inheritance in the kingdom of Christ
> and of God. Let no one deceive you with empty words, for
> because of these things the wrath of God comes upon the
> sons of disobedience. Therefore do not become partners
> with them (Eph. 5:3-7).

Language could not be plainer. Those who will not turn
from such sins have nothing to look forward to but the
wrath of God. Anyone who denies that is speaking 'empty
words.' Don't be deceived!

Let us go back a letter in the New Testament. Paul is
writing to the Galatians and says to them:

> Now the works of the flesh are evident: sexual immorality,
> impurity, sensuality, idolatry, sorcery, enmity, strife, jeal-
> ousy, fits of anger, rivalries, dissensions, divisions, envy,
> drunkenness, orgies, and things like these. I warn you, as
> I warned you before, that those who do such things will
> not inherit the kingdom of God (5:19-21).

No word here about a loss of rewards. It is the kingdom
itself that will be denied us.

Then, as a final reference, our Saviour's words in his
Sermon on the Mount:

> Not everyone who says to me, 'Lord, Lord,' will enter the
> kingdom of heaven, but the one who does the will of my

Father in heaven. On that day many will say to me, 'Lord, Lord, did we not prophesy in your name, and cast out demons in your name, and do many mighty works in your name?' And then I will declare to them, 'I never knew you; depart from me, you workers of lawlessness.'

Notice especially the denial that our Lord ever knew them. These are not people who were once saved but afterwards lost their salvation. They were never saved in the first place, notwithstanding both their profession and their Christian service.

There is an all-important truth that lies at the heart of this issue. It can be simply stated: the mark of a *true* Christian is holiness. Paul writes that 'if anyone is in Christ, he is a new creation. The old has passed away; behold, the new has come' (2 Cor. 5:17). This is not to suggest perfection. God's new creations are not yet complete! But if we have truly been united to Christ things have radically changed. The old life in which sin held sway has passed away. And if it hasn't, if sin is evidently still in charge it is a sign that we are not in Christ at all. We lack the identifying mark of the true Christian, namely, the holiness that expresses itself in a life of obedience.

Our subject calls us, then, to self-examination. How are we living? Is there some aspect of the will of God that we are knowingly, deliberately, habitually disobeying? We need to repent. It is just such behaviour that takes people to hell. Obedience is what separates the genuine from the false. If we lack it, God's urgent call is that we turn from our sin and seek his mercy.

This is not to deny that true Christians can fall into serious sin and remain impenitent for a time. The Bible makes plain that solemn possibility. I dare not say to anyone in that position, 'your sin is proof that you have never been born again.' But I can say, and must say, that for as long as one continues in sin one lacks the basic mark of the true believer. Such people have no grounds for thinking that they are truly saved. They need immediately to repent.

And what if by the grace of God we are *persevering* in obedience, repenting and returning to the Lord as often as we fall, eager to live a holy life however poor a job we feel we are making of it? We may humbly, yet joyfully, take it as evidence that the Lord, and his salvation, are truly ours!

13

Finished at Last!

The opening two chapters of Genesis allow us to be onlookers. We get to watch God at work as he adds more and yet more to his developing world as one creation day succeeds another. Eventually he finishes. Then he stands back as it were, examines it all, and pronounces it with deepest satisfaction to be 'very good' (Gen. 1:31). It is a thrilling picture: God making a beginning, carrying things on from day to day, bringing it all at last to glorious completion.

With salvation we have something similar, only more thrilling: God starting, continuing, and eventually finishing his work of saving sinners. Note the use of creation language: 'For God, who said, "Let light shine out of darkness," has shone in our hearts to give the light of the knowledge of the glory of God in the face of Jesus Christ' (2 Cor. 4:6); 'Therefore, if anyone is in Christ, he is a new creation' (2 Cor. 5:17); 'you were taught ... to put on the new self, created after the likeness of God in true righteousness and holiness' (Eph. 4:24). In saving us God is doing something like what he did at creation. And just as his creating work came to the most magnificent climax, so it will be with his saving. God is not going to stop short. The day is coming when he will present us 'blameless before the presence of his glory with great joy' (Jude 24).

The Scripture proof of this is so copious that a sample must suffice. Of his sheep, for example, Jesus says, 'I give them eternal life, and they will never perish, and no one will snatch them out of my hand' (John 10:28). Or here is what Paul says in his letter to the Philippians: 'And I am sure of this, that he who began a good work in you will bring it to completion at the day of Jesus Christ' (Phil. 1:6). In his first letter to the Corinthians the same apostle speaks of 'the revealing of our Lord Jesus Christ, who will sustain you to the end, guiltless in the day of our Lord Jesus Christ' (1 Cor. 1:7, 8). Then there is the closing section of Romans 8. Truth is piled on truth in order to persuade believers of the certainty of heaven. And right at the top, the assurance that nothing 'will be able to separate us from the love of God in Christ Jesus our Lord' (Rom. 8:35-39).

The implications of this for holiness are clear, and so encouraging. For making us holy is a major part of what God is doing in saving us. If therefore salvation as a whole is going to be completed that necessarily includes our sanctification. One day God will finish. He will reach his goal of conforming us to the image of his Son. For the saints who are now in glory that goal has been reached already. Hebrews describes them as 'the spirits of the righteous made perfect' (Heb. 12:23). The very same perfection is in store for all the rest of God's people. Death will rid us at last of the sin that remains in our hearts. At the resurrection God will clothe us with new bodies. Then afterwards, and to all eternity, we will live holy and God-pleasing lives in the new world he is going to make for us.

Beautiful there

Let us make a visit to that new world. If the opening two chapters of the Bible allow us to be onlookers, the last two chapters enable us to be visitors. In Revelation 21 and 22, John is sharing with us his vision of the new world of the future. With the help of our imaginations we can go there with him. What do we see? Here is one thing: we shall be *beautiful* there:

> Then I saw a new heaven and a new earth, for the first heaven and the first earth had passed away ... And I saw the holy city, new Jerusalem, coming down out of heaven from God, prepared as a bride adorned for her husband ... Then came one of the seven angels who had the seven bowls full of the seven last plagues and spoke to me, saying, 'Come, I will show you the Bride, the wife of the Lamb.' And he carried me away in the Spirit to a great, high mountain, and showed me the holy city Jerusalem, coming down out of heaven from God, having the glory of God, its radiance like a most rare jewel, clear as crystal (Rev. 21:1, 2, 9-11).

John is seeing two things here: a bride and a city. Yet marvellously they represent just the *one* thing, namely, the church. The vision is of the people of God as a whole. And it is a vision of beauty. The bride is adorned for her husband; the city is radiant with the glory of God. We shall be beautiful there! One reason for that will be our resurrection bodies. According to the apostle Paul, 'we await a Saviour, the Lord Jesus Christ, who will transform our lowly body to be like his glorious body' (Phil. 3:20, 21). Nothing of the sickness, weakness, and ageing that so ravage our bodies now will ravage them then.

And then to that outward splendour we add the inward. The beauty of holiness; the perfect likeness to Christ which is the object of God's sanctifying work; all the fruit of the Spirit and all of it fully ripe. Christ's goal in giving himself up for the church was 'that he might present the church to himself in splendour, without spot or wrinkle or any such thing, that she might be holy and without blemish' (Eph. 5:27). Evidently, that goal has at last been achieved.

Beautiful as a church

John's vision, as we have noted, is not of the individual believer but of the Lord's people together. What he is seeing is the glorified *church*. But the individual, of course, is an all-important contributor. If even one member were imperfect it would mar the beauty of the whole, just as one stain on a bride's dress mars the dress as a whole. The church of the future will be entirely spotless precisely because God has finished his saving work in each constituent member.

The contrast with the present is sharp and painful. Whether we are looking at the church in its local or wider expressions, beauty is by no means absent. The Spirit of God is at work and there is much in the church that is both lovely and honouring to her divine head: the beauty of holiness; the beauty of selfless, Christ-like love. But the beauty is marred. False teaching mars it. Tolerated sin mars it. Unacceptable worship mars it. Broken relationships mar it. Unconverted members mar it. Lovelessness mars it. The church of today is not remotely the object of beauty that our Saviour wishes and intends. But one day it will reach its goal! One day he will have the church for which he died. That is what we are seeing in Revelation 21: believers in Jesus will appear beautiful as a church because every imperfection in every member has been removed.

Beautiful because of Christ

In Revelation 22:14 a blessing is pronounced on 'those who wash their robes, so that they may have the right to the tree of life and that they may enter the city by the gates.' John is picking up on an earlier vision in which he sees the glorified saints wearing white robes. Why white? 'They have washed their robes and made them white in the blood of the Lamb' (Rev. 7:14). The picture is of a people made pure through the sacrificial work of Christ on Calvary. This is what gives them the right to the tree of life. This is what allows them to enter the city by the gates. It ties in with the words from Ephesians 5 quoted above. Christ's goal is to have a church 'without spot or wrinkle or any such thing,' but 'holy and without blemish' (Eph. 5:27). How does he obtain it? By giving himself up for her (Eph. 5:25). For our beauty in heaven, both as individual believers and as a church, we are indebted to the love that took Christ to the cross.

We may contrast this beauty with that which Adam and Eve had when they came from the Creator's hand. As with the citizens of the future world the outward and the inward, the physical and the spiritual, were entirely without flaw. God the divine artist, God the divine sculptor, had brought the most magnificent skills to the task and the end-product was a thing of exquisite beauty. But more was required to restore our beauty than the skills of the artist and sculptor. It was necessary that our Saviour shed his blood for us. Our future beauty will be to the praise not just of his remarkable creativity but of his amazing Calvary love.

Beautiful with the glory of God

The 'holy city Jerusalem' is described as 'having the glory of God, its radiance like a most rare jewel' (Rev. 21:10, 11). The church will have the stamp of God upon it. What we are will speak volumes about him, about his greatness. We will radiate his power, for example. If it can be said of us now that we are 'fearfully and wonderfully made' (Psa. 139:14), how much more when clothed in our resurrection humanity? Paul is explicit on this point. He speaks of the body as sown in dishonour, raised in glory; sown in weakness, raised in power (1 Cor. 15:43). And then, as the crown of it all, there is what we will be inwardly; in the perfection of holiness. How the goodness and the love and the grace and the holiness of God will shine out of us, to his eternal praise!

Beautiful forever

Scripture does not tell us how long it was before our first parents fell; only that they did. Satan was permitted to enter the Garden of Eden and successfully tempt them. And it changed everything. Their bodies became liable to death. They ceased to be holy. In a word, they lost their original beauty. But history is not destined to repeat itself. The vision of Revelation 21 is of a city into which nothing unclean will ever enter (Rev. 21:27). Satan has been cast into the lake of fire (Rev. 20:10). So too 'the cowardly, the faithless, the detestable … murderers, the sexually immoral, sorcerers, idolaters, and all liars' (Rev. 21:8). The new world will be a *safe* place to be. The holiness that cost our Saviour so much to obtain will never be in danger of being lost. It will be ours in perfection from the beginning. It will continue to be ours to all eternity.

Conclusion

The apostle Paul had a desire to depart and to be with Christ. It would, he was persuaded, be 'far better' (Phil. 1:23). You can readily understand why. Death would free him from sin and enable him to love and serve his Saviour in the way he so much wished to do. It is a big part of why death is 'gain' (1:21) for the believer. It is the door to perfect holiness.

But there is something better than death. Saints in heaven now are wonderfully free from sin but their salvation is not yet complete. Nor are they living in their final home, the promised new world. For that there needs to be the return of Christ. Only then will the vision of Revelation 21 and 22 be realized. That being so we end this chapter – and this book – with a prayer. It comes from the very chapters we have been looking at. Jesus says, 'Surely I am coming soon.' And John's response? 'Amen. Come, Lord Jesus!' (Rev. 22:20). Let that be our response too!

Further Reading

Where to Start

Albert N. Martin, *Living the Christian Life* (Edinburgh: Banner of Truth Trust, 1986)

J. C. Ryle, *Holiness* (Edinburgh: Banner of Truth Trust, 2014)

Kevin DeYoung, *The Hole in our Holiness* (Wheaton, IL: Crossway, 2012)

J. I. Packer, *A Passion For Holiness* (Wheaton, IL: Crossway, 1995)

In More Detail

Sinclair B. Ferguson, *Devoted To God: Blueprints for Sanctification* (Edinburgh: Banner of Truth Trust, 2017)

David Powlinson, *How Does Sanctification Work?* (Wheaton, IL: Crossway, 2017)

John Murray, *Collected Writings, Volume 2*, Section V (Edinburgh: Banner of Truth Trust, 1977)

John Owen, *Works, Volume 6, Temptation and Sin* (Edinburgh: Banner of Truth Trust, 1977)

The Bigger Picture

John Newton, *Letters of John Newton* (Edinburgh: Banner of Truth Trust, 2007)

John Murray, *Redemption Accomplished and Applied* (Edinburgh: Banner of Truth Trust, 2016)

J. I. Packer, *Keep in Step with the Spirit* (Leicester: IVP, 1984)

John Murray, *Principles of Conduct* (London: Tyndale Press, 1957)

Banner Mini-Guides

The Bible: God's Inerrant Word
Derek W. H. Thomas

The Christian Mind: Escaping Futility
William Edgar

The Church: Glorious Body, Radiant Bride
Mark G. Johnston

Growing in Grace: Becoming More Like Jesus
Jonathan Master

Regeneration: Made New by the Spirit of God
David B. McWilliams

Salvation: Full and Free in Christ
Ian Hamilton

Sanctification: Transformed Life
David Campbell